RAISED
— ON —
ROOFTOPS

Life Lessons from a Roofer's Daughter

CARI SMITH

Published by hope*books
2217 Matthews Township Pkwy
Suite D302
Matthews, NC 28105
www.hopebooks.com

hope*books is a division of hope*media

Printed in the United States of America

First paperback edition.
Paperback ISBN: 979-8-89185-320-1
Hardcover ISBN: 979-8-89185-321-8
Ebook ISBN: 979-8-89185-322-5
Library of Congress Number: 2025945684

DEDICATION

To Jay,

who loved me when I was on and off the roof,

and who helped us build our own.

I love you always and forever.

TABLE OF CONTENTS

Dedication .... *iii*

Thank You .... *vii*

Introduction .... *xi*

ON THE ROOF: LESSONS AS A DAUGHTER 1

    Our Barn – Our Story 3

    One Swift Swing of the Hammer 13

    Driver's Training 19

    Mausoleum 27

    Rooftop Judge 33

    Wrong Order 39

    Three Square Feet An Hour 47

    Value 57

OFF THE ROOF: LESSONS AS A WIFE 63

    Dust Bunny Rebellion 65

    Soup on Sundays 71

    Timing 77

    The Insurance Bill 81

    Strep Throat 87

    Dwelling.. 91

    Half-Marathon: 13.1 Miles 107

Alleluia Day 129

Excellent Customer Service.................................... 133

Best Hair Day 139

Funerals.. 147

BECOMING THE ROOF: LESSONS AS A MOTHER.......... 159

Eternity 161

Giggles.. 163

Sorry... 169

Bedtime 175

The Game 181

Peace... 185

Tatchos 193

Poking and Prodding 195

Dream Park... 199

Popcorn 207

Breakfast Story.. 213

Folding Clothes 215

Roofing Son.. 221

Life Lessons from the Peaks and Valleys 225

BOOK CLUB EXERCISES FOR EACH SECTION 229

1. Childhood and Family Projects........................... 229

2. Adulthood and Life Lessons.............................. 230

3. Motherhood and Perspective 230

4. General Bonus Exercise..................................... 231

THANK YOU

To the teachers who taught me to love words, story, and the rules of grammar, especially Mrs. Halfman, Mrs. Shauver, Mrs. Fox, and Spals.

To Janet Swenson—who first said she considered my stories literature, as they left her thinking about them long after I shared them.

To my Cohort and the rest of the 2010 Red Cedar Writing Project Group. You encouraged me when I thought I was writing a short story about my dad and realized partway through the class that I was working on a memoir.

To my regular writing crew, Mitch Nobis, Kristine Brickey, and the late Julie Achtenburg, as well as the many others who listened to and offered thoughts, asked probing questions, and suggested ideas for my writing at the Red Cedar Advanced Writing Institute every summer. Thank you for talking about my book as if it were a real entity when I still considered it a dream.

To my super early readers, Chad Walden and Heather Bennett, who spent time looking at my whole collection while it continued to grow. Your positive feedback, solid questions, and gentle prodding helped push me to dig deeper and connect each story.

To my middle school students who were exposed to some of these stories in their early and middle drafts, who encouraged me to keep writing, and who challenged me to be brave with my story. May this book inspire you and others to be courageous enough to tell your own story.

To my beta readers, Uncle Jay Schneider, Haley Thelen, and Brenda Halfman. You each were supportive and encouraged positive changes to this book. A special shout out to my dear friend Melanie Johnston-Butts, a wordsmith in her own right, who knows me well enough to ask challenging questions, push me when I need it, and snort laugh in the places I hoped she would.

To my publishing group at hope*books: Brian Dixon, Hope Dover, Kristin Osborn Neighbarger, Gloria Day, Amanda McMullen, and the many supportive writers I met along the way. Thank you for helping me make this dream a reality during the publishing process.

To my family, the ones I grew up with who grace these pages, to those whose stories are not yet written, and to those who chose to join our unique bunch. Thank you for helping me grow into the person I am and for being the cast and crew of my life.

To my boys, who most clearly helped me to understand the value of my upbringing: my parents, my brothers, our business, and our story. May you take these memories, learn your own lessons, and write your own story. Your mom loves you always and forever.

To my husband Jay, who always believed in me and this project. Who has been with me as a constant supporter and cheerleader. Who raises his eyebrows at me—I had no idea how critical they have been to our style of communication. Who shares all of life with me. Who has loved me, in all of my stages. Thank you. I love you. Always.

INTRODUCTION

In June of 2010, as a participant in the Red Cedar Writing Project at Michigan State University, I wrote a couple of stories about my dad during the first week of the institute. My father was a frequent character in the stories I wrote while I was at Michigan State. I was the daughter of a roofer, a man who was patient, practical, and quotable. He took his children to work, talked about life, taught them skills, and showed them how to live. It didn't take long for me to realize that while I was writing about him, I was also simultaneously discovering things about myself. My stories developed and took on a life of their own. As I heard feedback and encouragement to write, I decided that I would write a book, a memoir. It would probably take me about a year to finish.

Later that summer, I discovered I was pregnant—with our third son.

Life, it seemed, would happen to me and around me despite my lofty plans. Our family grew and I continued to write stories about my life as they continued to happen. I would file them away in the recesses of my mind to ponder and marinate. My book idea seemed to be too far-fetched and too demanding to happen while our life was unfolding. However, once a year, with encouragement from my husband, we hired a babysitter for an entire week, and I would leave the house daily to write.

My three children were frequently annoying, overwhelming, ridiculous, adorable, and hilarious. I sometimes posted short stories on Facebook, where our friends and families got a glimpse into our house and our family life. There was encouragement to keep writing. I wanted to remember the moments, and people seemed to enjoy them, so I wrote on.

Eventually, life got really challenging, as it often does. It seemed my parents and the other adults in my life got increasingly smarter as my children grew, and I experienced some of life's hardships. Memories of confusing statements said by the adults in my life started to make more sense. The lessons they tried to impart long ago were unfolding as difficult events in my life forced me to remember their advice. I sometimes wrote just to try to make sense of what was going on in my life. I wrote to process my emotions and, in doing so, learned yet even more lessons about myself and the wisdom of my elders. Their example was something to learn from and lean on as I found my own way in the world.

As the years moved on, the Facebook posts slowed. My then-middle schoolers were less excited about people getting a glimpse into our home life. It became more of a threat that I would "tell the people on Facebook" if they didn't stop misbehaving, which turned out to be an effective parenting move. My children developed their own interests and talents, requiring me to drive them around, so I only periodically made time to write. Eventually, the collection of stories grew into a body of work, though, evolving as its author did, developing a depth and structure not possible for my younger self to write without the life experience to build upon.

Again, for a while there wasn't much writing happening due to a job change, aging in-laws, Covid, two funerals, the selling of an estate, and our children's sporting events. Life happened. Lessons were learned and stored away until the time was right.

In the summer of 2024, I was drinking coffee with my then eighty-year-old mother, who had been hearing about this book idea since its infancy in 2010. I was talking about writing again. She, in her very German-tough-love-way, said, "Am I going to get to read this thing before I die?" which was the final push I needed to make my long-time dream a reality.

While this story is mine, dear reader, it is also for you. I hope you find within its pages glimpses of yourself. Learning about life from the vantage point of a rooftop is unique, as is being a roofer's daughter. However, many of the lessons, both on and off the rooftop, are, I hope, entertaining, poignant, and relatable. May you laugh. May you (maybe) cry. May these stories encourage you to think about your own life and the lessons you've learned. May you look for joy in the small moments. May you live with intention. May you give and receive love, as it is the best and most important thing life has to offer.

ON THE ROOF:

LESSONS AS A DAUGHTER

OUR BARN – OUR STORY

Clare Koenigsknecht wasn't born in a barn, but his earliest memories are of one. He's a storyteller, my dad. I grew up hearing about the farm down the road where his parents sharecropped for the first few years of his life until they purchased their own farm in 1949. That original farm, owned by Frank Bauer, had a traditional red barn with a gambrel-style roof raised in 1939, and it was there that my dad's stories began.

Many of my dad's childhood stories were set in that barn, and I loved to watch him tell them, his eyes brightening as he recalled the first memories of himself as a toddler. Even the wrinkles on his face seemed to fade as he launched into a story, churning up the past as a plough breaks old earth.

I grew up hearing stories of Dad in the hayloft, how he used to watch his father milk cows from the light of two lanterns his mom hung while the chores were completed. She washed the globes every day. From the haymow, he watched as his father butchered a cow—slaughtering, skinning, slicing—the resulting hunks of meat sent into the house to become food for the table, along with the morning's milk.

He remembers the changes, too, like the day his father brought home the tractor, and Nellie and Queenie, the team of field horses, were retired. They were loaded onto a truck, their leather work harnesses hung on the side. Later, in 1948, he'd come out of the haymow to watch electricity being installed, and, if I know my father, he was likely asking lots of questions when the electrician turned to him and said, "If you don't stay out of my way, I'll bury you under that stack of hay."

Nearly sixty years later, Dad heard that the current owner of his childhood barn, located less than a mile away from my childhood family's residence, was going to replace it with a pole building, and these memories came flooding back. One of his employees at the time said, "You should move it to your place." Dad listened and chuckled, the seed of an idea planted.

My dad didn't stay a farmer. Instead, he had become a self-employed roofer, specializing in flat roofs using the Conklin roofing system, though he was also known to shingle and find tricky leaks in valleys. In addition, he had done quite a bit of barn restoration, so he had the tools and knowledge needed to make the suggestion a reality. The planning and work involved in moving the almost seventy-year-old 76x32-foot barn would be a monumental undertaking. However, the thought of watching as the barn containing so many of his childhood memories being burnt or torn down became unthinkable. He pursued the crazy idea.

Crazy is the exact word Mom used when he approached her with the thought. My parents had always taught us that you invest in things that have meaning and value. To many outsiders, the money spent to move the barn could have easily been used to build something new. It was obvious after very little discussion, however, just how much Dad valued the barn and all the memories associated with it. "When he had his heart set on moving it here, it didn't bother me," was Mom's response. The investment began.

Phone calls were made to all five of us children. Dad's business was a family affair, each of us starting as early as five years old and helping out for many years. We learned many lessons, our foundation, while working together—the value of hard work, family cooperation (not always an easy message to absorb), and working toward a common goal. Over the years, we siblings learned unique skills and developed an affinity for restoration. Each of us had witnessed other people's joy, wonder, and deep gratitude when we restored their barn from a dilapidated structure to the beautiful functioning building of their memories.

Once, when an older couple employed Dad and our family to restore their barn, there was a happy, tearful reaction at the beauty of the newly restored barn, the center of their lives while farming. This understanding of the value of a barn, and the family that lived there, along with Dad's memories, made the news to move the Bauer barn the only logical choice. We knew our dad and understood his desire to preserve not only the building, but also the memories it contained. We were going to move the barn.

The thought of a family project quickly became the main topic of conversation during visits and phone calls. All of us would be together again working on a common goal, making new memories while reliving old ones. Dad hooked cables across the barn to stabilize it for when it traveled down the road. A moving company was hired. They laid two 80-foot steel beams placed lengthwise along the floor and six 40-foot cross beams placed intermittently to form the base for travel. There was 6x6-inch blocking from the metal beams to the rafter beams. The barn was then jacked up on iron and cribbing with dollies on one end and a Mack truck hooked on the front to pull the barn slowly to its new home.

Not only was there a great deal of work to get the barn itself ready, but there were many other logistical projects that needed tending to. The initial plan was to take the barn through the fields connecting the two locations, but the ground did not freeze the year before. We had visions of the barn hopelessly buried in a muddy sea, a red ship unfortunately beached in a sea of summer wheat, so it was decided the barn would travel down the road instead. There were power lines in the way, though, and any number of branches would prevent the 41-foot-wide load from traveling safely. Phone calls were made to the electrical company, dates were planned, and neighbors were informed of the project and how it would affect them. Kyle, the first child to help with the barn moving and the youngest son in his senior year at Michigan State University, came home and spent time with Dad trimming branches.

On December 3, 2008, the Bauer barn began its journey to its new home. There were visits from some of Dad's siblings, excited to see a part of their childhood restored and to witness its move—memories both remembered and preserved. The actual journey took three days. On the first day, the wires were cut between the barn and the road. The tractor-trailer inched down the driveway. On day two, Keith, the second youngest, came home to take pictures as the great structure crossed the ditch and lumbered down the road. The sight of a huge building, pulled by a semi on the road, toyed with the brain synapses of those who were watching. It was both amazing and unbelievable, even as you knew your eyes weren't playing tricks on you. Once on the road, the journey only took fifteen minutes. Mom stayed on the corner to stop traffic from interfering, a friendly face smiling and pointing at the obvious traffic obstruction. It would be another two hours, however, until the barn was in the field and off the road. Mom then retired from her traffic controller job and headed home. She wanted to make sure there was a warm lunch for the workers, always a much-looked-forward-to portion of the day, as her traffic directing skills were no match for the ones she used in the kitchen. The barn made the final leg of the trip on day three in the bitter cold, and was placed in its temporary resting place.

Once the barn arrived, Dad's vision started to take shape. The barn sat atop the beams and cribbing until the spring thaw when footings could be dug and a foundation set. Dad's eldest brother, Bill, came to help. The foundation was poured. The barn was set firmly in place.

Over the next three years, the barn became not only a place to house Dad's memories, but a place for my brothers and me to make our own. At the time, all of my brothers lived out of town, a couple of them out of state. Despite the distance, we all came home to work on the barn in its various stages of restoration. Everyone had a part in the painting. Tony, the second child and oldest boy in the family, was living in Texas, but made a trip home to work for a few days in 2009 as the barn was prepped to paint, old paint was scraped off, new blisters were created, and broken boards were replaced. Roger, the middle child, also came to work for a day from his residence in Ferndale, MI, cleaning dirt and creating sweat along with new memories. Keith, Kyle, and I pulled on our old work clothes (including a well-worn Fowler Football sweatshirt found in the closet), grabbed a roller, and painted at various times over the following weeks.

The large barn required us to brush off both our work skills and encouraged us to resume our sibling banter. We couldn't help but be reminded of our summers on the rooftop with the periodic mis-hit of the hammer (resulting in curses) and the need for a Band-Aid from an errant "diddly knife," known to the rest of the world as a utility knife. The monotonous spraying and rolling of primer brought back memories of the frequent boredom of the jobs we worked on when we were younger, which encouraged the use of our imagination to keep us entertained, sometimes in the form of sibling insults. "You still need someone to double-check your work, don't you, Rog?" I said, now with more teasing and less irritation than yesteryear, which brought on smiles and returned jabs to his sister.

Mom, the ever-supportive and multi-talented wife, did more than her fair share of barn work as well—each nailhead was primed to prevent rust, the trim painted bright white, a barn door built with Dad, and numerous meals were prepared for those who came to help. While we had all grown up and moved to different locations, we came home—to work, to share stories, and to create memories— together.

On the inside, there was work being done as well. I brought my children, then ages three and one, to check it out as the preparation for the cement floor was coming to a close. My oldest son, Tristan, inquisitive like his grandpa, asked question after question about what this was for and what that did. He was warned to stay away from a pile of wood meant to be eventually repurposed, nails still sticking out, which was likely to get him into trouble. Watching all the others working, he asked, "What can I do, Papa?" Dad gave him a job moving some boards out of the way, as there was work to be shared for those who were willing, regardless of age. Tristan smiled as he worked, feeling a sense of purpose. I smiled as well, watching my own son learn the satisfaction of being a part of things and of a job well done, a lesson that had served me well in adulthood. It seemed as though any family member who entered this special space made memories.

The paint job was finished, and the cement floor was seasoned; winter set in. We discussed further plans. The family's lift truck was parked in its new place, and the new space in both the bottom of the barn and the mow became useful again, storing barn wood, tools, and other assorted items needed for future barn preservation projects.

The barn was looking better than it ever had. So good, in fact, that Tony asked if he and his soon-to-be-bride could have their wedding reception there the following summer. Memories of working on the Family Barn Project were expected, but the suggestion of parties, family, and fun was an additional opportunity to add another layer of happy experiences. In preparation for the reception, the rafters were vacuumed of the decades of dust laying on them and antique tools were hung on the walls. A group picture of those in attendance, the barn as its canvas, was taken from the top of the lift truck. The story of the barn was told, the space enjoyed, another memory made by our family, and by those we loved who were in attendance.

Night fell, and the party continued. From the haymows where my father observed as a child, white paper globes bobbed in the breeze, and the rafters were illuminated by spotlights while the spelt in the field blew gently. Looking out at the field, the open barn door became a picture frame of our childhood backyard, revealing the beauty that had always been ours to enjoy. It seemed as though the barn was meant to be there—helping us to see the foundation laid for us by our family, bringing us together to work and play, giving us a unique view of the world.

The barn continued to be used. It would eventually store barn wood to be used for the restoration of other barns, a tractor, and a couple of projects in various stages of completion. We hosted a thirty-year reunion for all of the workers who had been a part of the family business, as the first party was such fun that we wanted to have another. Dad's business always focused on the people and the relationships of those we worked with, both the workers and the customers. It was another night of stories and memories.

The final addition was the new metal roof. I was sad to see the cedar shingles go, as I loved the character they added to the barn. Dad, however, wanted to make sure that it was sufficiently maintained to last another seventy years. There were more days spent working together, as most of the siblings made it home to tear off the existing roof or put on the new one. It was bittersweet to work side by side with Dad, as it was a reminder of times past when we were both younger. As we moved toward the end of the roof, however, it was also a reminder that our times of working together on family projects were likely limited, as we were both older, and the restoration was quickly coming to an end. We would have the barn, though, and the memories it contained.

The barn had become more than a structure for us. It began holding the stories of my father's childhood, his story. When we supported the idea of moving the barn, we invested in and built upon the foundation my parents worked to instill in us as we grew and worked together. Our family has a unique set of skills as a result of my father's business. We value working together and make it a point to do so, as it is a part of our family culture. We genuinely enjoy spending time with each other to create something to share with others. It is both the hard work *and* the celebrations connected to the barn that are valued, as enjoying the journey and the effort spent along the way are equally important parts. Growing up, this fact was commonplace, even mundane. As we have grown older, however, my siblings and I have started to realize the great value of this special gift, our unique view of the world. At the end of the day, it is still a big red barn. To my family and me, however, it is a source of pride and a symbol of what we value most—our family story.

ONE SWIFT SWING
OF THE HAMMER

The hammer felt heavier with every nail. Sweat gathered at the back of my neck, trickling down between my shoulder blades as the sun climbed higher in the sky. I wiped my brow with the back of my hand and squinted at the rows of trusses stretching above me. This was supposed to be summer vacation. Other kids were at the pool or sleeping in, but I was stuck on this roof, building a garage I didn't care about with my dad and brothers—none of whom I liked very much at the moment.

My father was a roofer who *loved* a good family project. He valued the family bonding time and work ethic it gave to his kids. It gave him opportunities to talk about life lessons and interact with us on a level most dads didn't. *"Hard work pays off," "Learning new things is good for you and will help you in the future,"* and *"Learning to work with other people* (annoying younger brothers included) *is a priceless skill"* were just a few of the gems I heard on a regular basis. I usually enjoyed our time together. However, as I lined up another nail and swung the hammer, missing the mark and smashing my thumb yet again, I silently wished he cared a little less about my character.

We built the garage from the ground up. We laid our own foundation (another not-so-happy-tale), framed it in, and put up the trusses. For anyone who hasn't had the pleasure of building their own garage or other large building, when the trusses are put up, a 2"x4" board is nailed across the beams lengthwise to space them appropriately and keep them in place until the 4'x8' sheets of ply-wood, which make the rooftop, are put into place. On this not-so-happy morning, it was my job to put nails at 8-10" intervals on the boards that were already tacked into place to firmly secure them to the trusses. It was not my favorite job, as my hand-eye coordination was not great—my thumb usually paid the price.

Tony, my brother two years my junior, on the other hand, al-ways got the easy jobs, and today was no exception. I had been wait-ing for days, perhaps weeks, to get the *easy* job. It seemed as though my age and experience, which my father had told me were going to help me in life, were my worst enemies. Every time I looked at Tony, he was just standing by Dad, waiting for the next piddly errand to run while I labored under the already hot sun, hammering away nail after nail after nail. This process was broken up only by the periodic missed hit, followed by yelling and cursing from me, and a stifled giggle by Tony, which only made me dislike him and his pathetic job even more.

As I nursed my throbbing thumb, I looked at him, glaring, and saw him get yet another easy job from Dad. I had been working hard all morning, and we were ready to add the next row of wood sheeting to the roof. Tony had been given instructions to pull up the 2x4s that had been holding the trusses to the appropriate spacing, but were now in the way. I smirked as he set to work. My job wasn't easier, as I had hoped, but at least Tony wasn't just standing there anymore. I, in the meantime, continued my monotonous job of nailing.

My pleasure increased, as it seemed Tony wasn't getting very far whenever I glanced back at him. *How hard could it be?* I thought. "What are you doing, Tony?" I taunted in his general direction. "Dad finally gives you a real job, and you can't even do it right?"

"Shut up, Cari. This is harder than it looks. I know *you* couldn't do it!" he yelled breathlessly back as he strained to pull out the first spike.

"Why would I want to? I've already got a job, and if you don't hurry up, I'll have to do your job for you, too. I've been doing everything all morning anyway," I retorted, rolling my eyes. I was so tired of his smart mouth.

As I got back to the task at hand, I noticed Tony switch strategies. He had been trying to dislodge the nails from the top of the 2x4 to no avail. He was now standing on the crossbeam of the rafter, facing the 2x4 that was about chest high to him. He had the hammer in both hands and was swinging it between his legs and up to the underside of the board in the hopes of lifting the board and the nail that held it in place, freeing it from the truss. I snidely thought, as my own thumb throbbed, *It sure would suck for him if he missed the board*. I turned my body slightly in morbid anticipation of the worst.

Not three hammer-swings later, my wicked intuition became reality. The board had started to get pretty loose, so Tony had started swinging harder. The next sequence of events unfolded like the action part of the movie when everything changes to slow motion, so you don't miss one detail of the best scene. I don't know if the board shifted or if Tony's aim was off, but as the hammer came up slowly from his legs into an arc toward his target, the next swing missed the board entirely.

The head of the hammer landed square—right between his eyes.

Hard.

He stood stunned at the blow. I could almost see the neurons firing as the signal of *extreme* pain shot through his nervous system. The slight delay made the scream that followed all the more intense. The hammer dropped silently to the ground below as Tony put both hands on his forehead to stop, or at least minimize, the throb that must have pounded within his head. While sudden death was out of the question, it seemed as though he was definitely going to have one heck of a headache.

Having left my compassion elsewhere that day, I laughed with as much vigor as my brother was crying with. It was quite possibly the funniest thing I had ever witnessed. Even today, that image makes me smile. I feel a bit evil and cold-hearted to say that, but it's the truth. If I couldn't get the easy job, this was a pretty good substitution. It was as if all of the unfairness of the day and the weeks prior to this event had suddenly vanished and had been made right again. Even my thumb felt better.

It was this scene, Tony crying as hard as I was laughing, that my father saw as he responded to the yell of my brother. "What the hell's going on over here?" Dad exclaimed as he came on the scene. I was initially blamed—as laughing at another's misfortune at our house usually meant you were to blame for the injury. I pleaded innocent and was found not guilty based mostly on proximity; I was too far away to have caused the injury. Tony was in such pain that finding fault was not as important as surveying the damage done and determining the next course of action.

As a result of his misfortune, Tony was excused from the day's labors, but that was okay. I had been waiting for the easy job. I still didn't have it. But I no longer had to watch Tony *do* the easy job all day, either. The day was hot, and the sun was unforgiving. My crap job remained crappy. My other family members continued to bug me.

Despite the sweltering heat, though, I remained on the roof working away and smugly smiling. I'm certain that Dad had a different lesson in mind for me to learn that morning than the one I walked away with, but this particular gem has served me well, too. "Life isn't fair" was a lesson taught often at my house, but "Good things happen to those who wait" was the one shouted from the rooftop that day with one swift swing of the hammer.

Driver's Training

"Try her again," said Dad, confident that with practice, I could learn the fine art of driving a stick shift. The Ford 350 idled in the road. I sat perched on the edge of the driver's seat, the only way I could reach the gas pedal, shifter in hand, feet on the clutch and the gas. I attempted to turn into the driveway again.

Sputter. Stall. Stop. We were getting nowhere fast.

I sighed heavily and looked to Dad for rescue despite knowing, based on many past experiences, we'd be here all day until I could figure out how to drive if that's what it took. The truck continued to sit in the road, poised for action. I tried again. Moving. Lurching. Stalling. Stopping. Much like a cat trying to cough up a hairball, only to realize that it was still stuck in its throat and doing the same retching action again. And again. We had probably been there for three minutes. It felt like three hours and would soon feel like three days. Perhaps we would be here all summer. Nevertheless, we were stuck on the road and had been for five straight attempts. My lesson in driving with a stick shift was not going well.

"I hate this," I muttered under my breath. "This" referred to any number of meanings: "I hate you for making me drive when I'm obviously not ready." Or "I hate the fact that the cutest guy you have ever hired is sitting next to me, and I am giving him whiplash." Or "I hate knowing that at any moment another car is going to come up behind me, and I'll feel even more pressure to get into the driveway." But mostly: "I hate feeling so incompetent."

I tried again. We heaved, jumped, and settled.

Staring straight out the window, willing my tears to stay behind my eyeballs, I spat, "What am I doing wrong?" I knew the answer: Everything. I was doing everything wrong.

"Just let up on the clutch a little slower and give it a bit more gas," came Dad's patient suggestion.

I wanted to vanish. Dad was sitting calmly beside me. "Lyle the Cute," in the meantime, was still sitting on the passenger side, a faint smirk on his face. From the corner of my eye, it looked as though it were a strange mixture of amusement, pity, and compassion, but mostly a desire for me to figure it out and get us into the parking lot. If not for my sake, then for the sake of his neck, which was being repeatedly and violently thrust forward and backward at speeds that could cause serious damage.

I was well aware that there was nothing impressive or appealing in my display of inept driving skills to attract his attention. Instead of him thinking, "Hey, she's cute, and I'd like to get to know her better," as I had hoped this summer, I'm pretty sure he was thinking, "I wonder if I can get Workman's Comp for my neck injury? It will be one of the more interesting stories they'll get, I'm sure."

I tried again.

By nature of a small miracle, we made it into the driveway. Finally, I was able to park without any unnecessary excitement. I turned off the engine. I breathed a sigh of relief. Lyle smiled and quietly said, "Good work."

I scoffed in obvious disagreement with his statement and escaped the confines of the truck. I set to work, grabbing a couple of hammers and unhooking the ladder. I had no idea what we were doing that day, but I hoped to get started as quickly as possible in order to rescue the day from its crap-tastic beginning. Lyle put up the ladder, while Dad looked for a power outlet. I was graciously allowed to privately pick up the pieces of my pride and attempt to duct tape them together, while everyone else got ready to start our day.

The initial set-up for the morning was complete. We all stood on the roof getting instructions from Dad. "Cari, you start here in the corner and pull out the tar. You'll be taping that later today. Lyle, why don't you come over here with me, and we'll get started tearing off the main section. Hopefully, we can get it sheeted and primed by mid-afternoon."

Dad seemed oblivious to the joy I felt at his directions. I would be left to myself, but perched in a perfect position to watch Lyle for most of the morning. Things were improving.

Dad finished his directions. Lyle smiled at me, asking, "Would you hand me that spud?"

His eyes—wow.

I was getting lost in his eyes; I think Debbie Gibson started singing.

I smiled.

He smiled.

He kept smiling and pointed. "The one over there."

"Oh... yeah... sure," my trance broke. I grabbed the tool and quickly handed it to him. I was becoming more thankful for my solitary job by the moment, as "Biggest Babbling Idiot" was not a title I wanted to earn today on top of my already clinched "Incompetent Driver" award.

About half an hour later, the ladder began bouncing and the owner's head popped up above the roof deck. "Good morning," he said, smiling at me.

"Good morning," I responded.

"Is Clare up here?" he asked. I pointed to the other end of the roof.

He noticed Dad, offered quick thanks to me, and went over to ask his questions. I got back to work, stealing quick glances at Lyle. My day was progressing nicely.

Shortly thereafter, Dad and the owner walked toward the ladder near my workspace. "Cari, this is Tom, and he owns this place."

"Good morning again, Tom. It's nice to meet you," I replied, not offering to shake hands but signaling at my tar-laden fingertips as my reasonable excuse.

"It's nice to meet you, Cari. Thanks for the entertainment this morning, by the way," he smiled at me. "We were watching out the front window during our staff meeting. We started taking bets to see how many times it would take for you to get into the driveway." I did not smile. I did, however, blush, realizing my audience had just grown dramatically. He climbed down the ladder still chuckling. I, meanwhile, wanted to die anew. The humiliation of this day had reached unprecedented levels.

I willed myself to death and continued pulling at the tar, working my way out of the corner while I waited. My imagination wandered as I began to think of the many other awful things that could happen to me today which might top the events of the morning. There weren't many options left. While death seemed to be avoiding me, an injury could keep it interesting. Blood and emergency lights, drawing further attention to my inadequacies, might top the negative attention I'd received so far. Though Lyle might have to carry me if I were to break my leg. I smiled.

Despite its best efforts, none of my imagination's wanderings came to fruition. The morning continued. I battled tar. Lyle remained cute. As the day wore on, I realized that it was becoming unlikely that I would die from humiliation, though a few short hours ago I had believed it was a certainty.

"I think we've done enough," Dad exclaimed late in the afternoon. "Let's pack it up and call it a day. Carl, why don't you drive us home?"

"Really?" I whined. My chest tightened in dread. "'Cause I was so good at it this morning?" I asked, voice dripping with sarcasm.

Dad got onto the ladder with a bucket of tools. "Oh, it wasn't that bad. And you won't get better if you don't practice," he said as his head disappeared, ending the conversation.

My father's and my definition of "that bad" were obviously

dramatically different. I knew two things: Dad would be calm and patient the entire ride home, giving helpful suggestions if asked. I could take as long as I needed. He wouldn't even mention it if he had to pay Lyle for an extra half an hour of work. I also knew that I would have to explain why we were late for dinner to all of my younger brothers. I groaned in frustration and fear. I got on the ladder with my load and looked at Lyle, who would follow me down. "I'm sorry in advance," I said.

He smiled. I couldn't resist smiling in return.

Truck loaded, I closed my eyes and sent a prayer heavenward. I comforted myself with the knowledge that there was no staff meeting, and Lyle couldn't think I was worse at driving than he already did. Perched on the edge of the seat, I pushed in the clutch, put the stick in reverse, and looked back, grateful that there was nothing I could run into behind us for quite a ways. I pushed on the gas, and we shimmied. With a bit of luck, we also went in reverse and did not stall. I let out the breath I didn't know I was holding and put the truck into first gear. Saying another prayer for good measure, I let out the clutch and pushed on the gas. We moved forward, creeping to the end of the driveway. I stopped, looked both ways. There were no cars coming.

I paused to gather my courage. Everyone waited. I let up on the clutch again, and we lurched forward. And lurched again. Our collective headbanging, sans music, continued as we lurched yet again. It was a rough start, but we did not stop. We gained speed. I shifted into second gear.

"Lookey there, you've got it!" Dad exclaimed as he settled in for the ride. I rolled my eyes, though I was secretly glad we made it out of the driveway.

Through divine intervention and forced repetition, I was able to drive home without stalling once. After we pulled into the driveway, I pushed in the stick one last time and turned off the engine. I breathed a sigh of relief. Lyle smiled and quietly said, "Good work." Dad also sighed contentedly, happy with the results of the day's driving lesson, and headed into the house for dinner.

MAUSOLEUM

"So, you're going to make sure you don't cut all the way through the board. We just want to bend it. Make sure it sits in this valley nice and smooth, but without creating a break in the wood," Dad explained. "Be sure to measure twice and cut once, 'cause I've got just enough board to get this part finished this morning." Tony and I, aged eleven and thirteen, stood side by side getting the day's directions. I was leery we were up for the task, but Dad seemed to have the utmost confidence.

On the drive to the job, located in a cemetery, Dad informed us, "They also keep bodies in there in the middle of the winter, stack 'em right up when the ground is too frozen to plant 'em." I hadn't figured out if he was kidding or not, but I didn't want to ask. I was also glad we were well into the summer season, so I wouldn't have to think about working with fresh corpses beneath us if he was telling us the truth.

"What if we mess it up? Where are you going to be?" I asked, realizing we were being given directions as though Dad would be elsewhere for the rest of the morning.

"Well," he paused, evidently not having thought of the possibility. "I guess we'll have to buy more wood after lunch. I've got to go look at a job for next week in Pewamo, so I'll be gone for a couple of hours. Measure twice. Cut once. Feel free to start on the flashing if you get done early. You've got to think like a drip, though I don't think our occupants will mind if they get wet." Dad chuckled at his own joke.

We arrived and started unloading. I looked to Tony to see if he felt as concerned by the day's task as I did. I waited for him to protest with me. He looked back and shrugged his shoulders. He seemed to be mentally trying to remember the list of tasks for the morning.

We stood atop the mausoleum in Muir Cemetery. It wasn't really a mausoleum, though. It was a flat-roofed storage shed, about 10'x15', meant to house the gardening tools. The roof surface was mostly flat, but the center of the roof was several inches below the edges from front to back, creating a small valley to allow for water drainage. The building was made of stone and had an ornate wooden door, though, so it seemed like a building with more grandeur than its purpose required.

I exclaimed, "You're leaving us here alone?" As we all stood on the roof, my concerns were realized and verbalized at the same time. "What do we do if someone asks about a couple of kids hanging out on the roof of the mausoleum?"

"I guess you explain it to them. You know what you're doing," he shrugged, unconcerned, and started down the ladder. "Measure twice and don't cut all the way through," he repeated as his head disappeared.

Tony and I stood quietly with our thoughts as we watched the truck drive away.

We stood there for another minute before turning to each other. We realized it was just the two of us. Not only had Dad left us here alone, but he also expected us to get the first part of this job done. In an attempt to get started, Tony asked, "Where's the tape measure?"

"You have to cut," I decided, appointing him the Power Tool User. "Dad is crazy, leaving us here to do this." I shook my head.

Though it sounded more like a pep talk than an actual conviction, he responded, "I think we can do it."

I chuckled, unconvinced, "I sure hope so. The tape measure is over there." I pointed. We set to work.

We had measured at least three times. Tony had plugged in the saw. The moment of truth was upon us. Cut—but not too deep—and hope the sheet of wood would fit in place like we hoped it would.

He was about to pull the trigger when I heard, "Hey! What in the hell are you kids doing up there?" I turned my head to see a middle-aged man walking our way, finger wagging in the air, reprimanding us while we looked at him from the rooftop.

"Awesome," Tony whispered to no one in particular.

"Yeah," I agreed, with equal sarcasm.

I stood up, rubbed my dirty hands on the side of my legs, and smiled. I turned to meet our visitor, hoping I could convince him we were not the delinquents of his suspicions. "Good morning, how are you?" I spoke in the most friendly, confident tone I could muster, waving as I walked to the end of the roof. "Come on up!" The words coming out of my mouth surprised me as much as they seemed to surprise our unannounced guest. Evidently, I was going to pretend I felt *way* more confident about the day's plan than I really did.

He paused one step, but continued walking our way and climbed the ladder. As his head reached roof level, his tone changed slightly, but he asked again, "What are you kids doing up here?" He paused at the top of the ladder, waiting for our response.

"Hi, I'm Cari, Clare Koenigsknecht's daughter, and this is Tony, his son. We were just getting ready to partially split this four-foot by eight-foot sheeting in order to get it to lay down nice and flat in this valley. We don't want to cut all the way through, as that will create an additional seam on the roof. We don't want any guests downstairs getting wet if we can avoid it," I smiled at him, while mentally hitting my head with the palm of my hand at the repetition of my dad's terrible joke.

He looked at me, unsure how to react.

I rambled on, "Once we get that secured, we are going to work on laying the flashing down along each wall. Later this afternoon, we will lay down the base coat on the whole thing and tape the seams on the flashing. You'll be watertight by nightfall," I continued, not able to stop myself from talking. I was impressed with how informed and confident I sounded. "I think Dad plans to be finished by the end of the week. It will be one solid, seamless, waterproof, white roof when we are done. It will last for years," I turned for confirmation from my brother. Tony nodded slightly in the background. I continued to smile, starting to feel like I was knowledgably in charge. Perhaps there was no need to *fake it 'till you make it* when you actually *did* know what you were doing.

I'm not sure what he expected, but it wasn't my answer. "Hmm," he grunted, unsure of how to proceed now that he realized we weren't hoodlums. He put out his hand, "Nice to meet you. I'm Sam Jones." We each shook his hand. "Would you have your dad give me a call when he gets a chance? I have a couple of questions for him."

"We sure will, Mr. Jones." I continued to smile, hoping he would leave before he changed his mind. "It was nice to meet you."

"You kids, too," and he waved, then climbed back down the ladder.

I took a deep breath. "That went better than expected," I said to Tony.

"Yeah, that was good. He looked really mad to start."

"We sound like real roofers, huh?" I smiled. We turned back to our work.

Dad arrived just before lunch, and we were excited to show him what we'd accomplished. We had gotten the sheeting into place as directed. Tony had needed to cut the plywood twice, but only because I was nervous about him cutting it too deep the first time. In the end, the decking lay pretty darn straight, requiring only one small additional piece of plywood to be put into the corner. We were working on the flashing as Dad climbed up the ladder.

"Well, lookie-here!" he exclaimed as his head rose above the roof's surface.

We smiled at his approval. "Sam Jones stopped by while you were gone," I told him. "He thought we were troublemakers at first, but I think we convinced him we knew what we were doing. He wants you to contact him about some questions he has."

"Yeah, he was yelling at us to start," Tony added.

"That's what I heard." He chuckled, "I ran into him when I pulled up. He said he saw some kids and thought they were causing problems, but he said he found out they were mine, and they seem to really know their stuff." He smiled, obviously proud that we had handled ourselves well. "See," he looked at me, "I told you you knew what you were doing."

Rooftop Judge

"You're a moron! That won't work," I screamed, exasperated. "Yes, it will! You won't even try. I'm doing it anyway," Roger yelled back as he rolled his eyes and drew back his hammer.

I knew our dad was going to be upset and would have to buy more supplies. I would get in trouble because I was the oldest—and because my younger brother was being an idiot. "We're doing it my way," I retorted as I moved to block him from going through with his terrible idea.

It had been a loud and unhappy morning on the rooftop. We were shingling the peak and redoing the flat portion of the roof of a former judge. Dad had left for a while to look at another job. Meanwhile, my brothers and I were left to fend for ourselves. We were in the middle of shingling the roof—the mindless portion where row by row was added one shingle and four nails at a time. What *should* have been a straightforward part of the job, though, had turned into a big argument.

While the morning had been relatively productive, it had been pretty painful as well. I had gotten stuck working with Roger—again. Tony was the row starter on the far end, cutting the first shingle of each row to the specified length, nailing it on, and moving on to the next row. Keith, the third youngest of the bunch, got stuck doing some cleaning on the flat roof beneath us; boring, but a job that included the luxury of working alone.

Roger and I weren't known for our ability to get along with each other. His "creative" thinking drove me crazy—not only because it was different from mine, and I was always right, but also because some of his less brilliant ideas had cost my father time and money. Being the oldest, I believed I was supposed to foresee the stupidity of his ways and felt I had taken the brunt of Dad's disappointment and frustration for poor ideas in the past. Unfortunately, Roger, the middle child, had had just enough workable, sometimes even good, ideas in the past to give him, in my mind, an over-inflated confidence in himself, which had made him bound and determined to make his idea work today.

Afraid of Dad's frustration and of having to fix our mistakes (including the hours it might take to correct), I was equally as determined to stop his terrible idea in its infancy. It was bad enough I got stuck working with Roger that morning—I was NOT going to be stuck working with him all afternoon fixing his hair-brained idea.

So we stood, yelling at each other. Doing nothing.

"I'm telling you that you're a moron, and I have no intention of letting you get your way with this idea," I yelled. "You want to run five rows of shingles, but we can't even get the spacing right when we do only two or three. I'll be damned if I have to spend all afternoon pulling up nails from hot, tar shingles—ruining half of them in the process, I might add—to fix an even bigger spacing issue than we have right now. I said, 'No,' and I'm not going to do it. If you want to take the top rows while I work on the bottom ones, fine. Actually, maybe that's better because then I won't have to work with you at all!"

"Listen, it's going to work," Roger commented as his frustration at my resistance continued. "We'll be able to move faster and scuff fewer shingles. My side of the shingle is always spaced right. Maybe if you'd do your job better and make sure your 5 inches is really 5 inches, then we could get this done faster. It's not like I *love* working with you either." He stood to face me.

My exasperation at his insistence on trying out his idea was only increasing as the temperature of the day continued to rise at as fast a rate as my temper. Interested in a second opinion, I turned and looked down at Keith. He not only had the unfortunate job of cleaning up this morning, but was also in a position to have overheard our entire discussion. "Keith, who do you think is right here? Don't you agree that Roger's idea is stupid and isn't going to work anyway? Tell him I'm right and he's a moron," I encouraged, confident that Keith would take my side. I saw Roger, out of the corner of my eye, shaking his head back and forth both in disgust at me and to discourage Keith from picking my side.

Keith briefly looked up, shook his head, and calmly replied, "I'm not picking a side. I think you're both idiots." He slowly turned his back to us and went back to picking up shingle pieces and sawdust. His refusal to get involved only added fuel to my fire.

I turned back to Roger as he continued our argument. "You

just don't like my idea because it's a good one, and you didn't think of it. You aren't the only one who can think of ideas. You always want to do things the slowest way possible. We can get more done in less time using my idea. If you'd have thought of it first, you would think this idea was brilliant! You just can't admit that I might be smarter than you!"

By the end of his monologue, he was yelling as loudly as I had been. We were as close to nose and nose as you could be on a slanted roof. I normally stood almost four inches higher than Rog, but he was standing a few feet above me, intentionally, so he could look into my eyes. It was clear that any productivity we may have had that morning was quickly going to the wayside. I wasn't going to go along with his ridiculous idea, and he wasn't going to let me deter him from an idea he now regarded as his best ever.

It was in this standoff position, then, that we found ourselves as Tony walked over and joined the discussion. "Do you guys have any idea how stupid you both sound?"

We turned to look at him, and I opened my mouth to respond.

"No, really," he stopped me with his hand in an effort to get me to listen. "Just listen to yourselves for a second. This is Dad's *business* and you two are yelling at each other. Not only can the person we're working for hear everything going on, but the four houses surrounding this place have to be able to hear you, too. We're working in town. You're *both* morons, *AND* you're making Dad look bad. I'm sure the owners don't expect a group of roofer's kids to act like total professionals, but they don't expect them to act like yelling, screaming idiots who can't get along and agree on much of anything. You're making us all look bad. Either idea will work. Pick one and quit screaming at each other." He walked away.

We both stood there. Stunned.

Even though I hated being told what to do, especially by a younger brother, I had a hard time arguing with his point. I really wanted to reply with some quick-witted comment, but nothing came to me. The verdict had come down—we were both acting immaturely. Not just Roger, as I had hoped, but I, too, was guilty as charged.

The irony of being on the rooftop of a former judge was, I believe, lost on me at the time, but as Tony's opinion on the situation sank in, I realized he was right. I had never thought to listen to myself as an outsider, as I had always been too involved in the argument, usually with Roger, to realize that he wasn't the only one yelling and screaming—sounding like a moron.

As Tony's words sank in, I found myself embarrassed not only for the fight that had just occurred, but for all of those noisy arguments that had happened this summer and last. There had been lots of them. Perhaps I wasn't as mature as I wanted to believe. I had always thought Roger was a stupid kid for yelling. If that was the measuring stick, then the label of "stupid" fit me as well. It hit me with the force of a hammer.

Once it was brought to my attention that others might be listening and passing judgment, I realized that the problem was less about how to do the job and more about how to interact with each other in a way that didn't make me, or my father's business, look bad. I had always prided myself on being a good communicator as well as doing a good job while in charge, but the case Tony presented against me made it pretty hard to argue. It had been brought to my attention that our ears weren't the only ones that might be listening to what was going on—not only on the roof, but whenever we were out in public. My brother, the rooftop judge, had found me guilty as charged.

I'd love to say that Roger and I never fought again and that we learned to solve our differences in a civil and efficient manner from that day forward. Anyone who's had a younger sibling would know I was lying. I don't even remember if we used Roger's idea or my own that afternoon. I imagine he rolled his eyes and thought evil thoughts about his older sister if my idea was the one we went with. If we used his idea, I'm sure I pretended not to notice the smug smile on his face and double-checked the spacing of the shingles frequently to ensure I wouldn't have to work one minute longer with him than necessary.

What I do remember from that day is the lesson: Others are watching and listening. What I do and say is a reflection not only on myself, but the team, family, or profession of which I am a part.

WRONG ORDER

As each of the twelve eight-foot long beams, measuring in at six inches by six inches and weighing in at about 100 pounds each, was laid in the truck bed one at a time, my stomach dropped like the back shocks in equal measure. I was becoming certain I did not order what Dad really wanted. I remained standing, however, silently watching them load what I was now sure was the wrong order into the truck. It in no way matched the job we were doing. The worker gave me the receipt. I thanked him and started the Ford F-350. *This isn't going to go well,* I thought as I pulled out of the drive and headed home.

We were working at home for a stretch that summer. It wasn't my favorite, because that meant sometimes we ate at home instead of at a restaurant, which was our usual routine and by far the best part of the day. There was also no travel time, so the workday was longer. We were also at home, so there were no people to watch, other than the annoying ones I lived with.

The day had dragged on, like so many others that week, when Dad said, "Hey, Cari, I need you to run to Wieber's and grab some more wood. We need twelve (something) two (something else)... eight pieces of...," he rattled off the order. In my eagerness to escape, I had stopped listening carefully once I was told I was going to get to go to town.

"Sure!" I said, hustling over to the ladder before he changed his mind and sent Greg, our hired help that day. "I'll be right back. Do I just charge it to the account?" I asked, as I descended.

"That will work," he said, as I disappeared from sight.

The drive to town was a short one. Wieber Lumber was the local lumber yard, supply store, and DIY place. Dad was a regular customer, and my brothers and I had been coming here with him for years. It was one of the only times I'd come in by myself, though, as I was a fairly new driver. I knew there would be no issue for me to order whatever was needed for the day. Everyone there knew who I belonged to—there would be no need to ask me for my ID, as Dad and I not only shared the same last name, but also the same nose and blue eyes.

I got to the counter and simultaneously realized that in my haste to leave the house, I hadn't been a very good listener. *There was definitely an eight in there. And a twelve. A six. Was there a two?* My thoughts became a bit frenzied as Dale, Wieber's lumber yard manager, a small man with a big personality, approached with his characteristic charming smile. "What can I do for you?" he asked as he pulled out a pen and the order tablet.

I smiled back, equalling his friendliness. "Hi, Dale. Good to see you," I stalled. "I need some wood for Dad today," knowing that part, at least, was correct. "And will you charge it to Dad's account?" adding in as much known detail before I needed to know before the actual order as possible.

"Will do. What do you need?" he asked again, pen still in the ready position.

Looking at the shelves of screws, nails, spray paint, and hammers, I paused. *I actually only sorta know*, I thought to myself, feeling smaller and less confident than I had on my way into town. I felt compelled to tinker with the cup of Phillips head magnetic screwdriver tips on the counter as I frantically considered what to do, all while trying desperately to look calm.

I continued to smile, though I'm sure it no longer reached my eyes.

I briefly considered asking to use the phone. The idea of waiting for Dad to come off the roof and answer my question while Dale watched me was quickly dismissed as terrible. Not only would it result in a tremendous amount of embarrassment on my part while we all waited, it would be a waste of Dad and Dale's time.

I'm pretty sure I remember. What's the worst that can happen?

I took a breath and hoped for the best. "I need some wood— twelve 6x6 boards, eight feet long," I ordered, still smiling. I was beginning to feel like the Cheshire cat.

Without hesitation, Dale filled in the form, totalled the bill, had me sign, and sent me on my way to collect the wood. I breathed a sigh of relief. Since he didn't look at me like I was ridiculous, I figured I must have gotten it right, as my collection of numbers and measurements actually existed out in the lumber yard. I had a receipt to prove it.

My confidence was short-lived, though. Once I pulled into the lumber yard and the worker had taken the paper, it wasn't long before my initial intuition that I'd gotten it wrong was confirmed. At first, I thought he had just misread the paper, as he headed toward the pile of beams, meant for frames and barns, and not toward the more house-project-looking pile I expected him to go to. I mentally went through what I had actually asked for, realizing that a 6x6 was indeed a big piece of wood. And I had ordered twelve of them.

Oh, hell.

I debated stopping him. But I didn't know what to ask for instead. And I didn't really want to go back inside to the counter to call the house to ask, which I had still decided was a level of embarrassment I wasn't willing to endure. It was either maintain my pride or face the anger of Clare. Or even worse, his disappointment. In the end, my indecision decided for me. While I was doing nothing but playing mental tug-of-war, the order had been all loaded. The worker gave me the receipt. I thanked him, started the Ford F-350, and headed home. *What have I done?* I thought as I pulled out of the drive.

As I drove over the hill and the house came into view, my suspicions became a certainty. There was no way we were using any of this wood on our house project. I had purchased barn wood; we were working on the roof.

Tears stung my eyes. I considered driving around the section to delay the inevitable. I'd likely been spotted already, though, so I drove the quarter mile past the corner and turned into the drive, parked in front of the house, and turned off the truck. I wiped my tears and readied myself to leave the truck, which I had finally learned to drive. I hadn't died of embarrassment in front of Lyle, but life seemed to be giving me a lot of second chances.

I took a deep breath.

Dad walked around the corner, confusion in his eyes. Frustration flared but was quickly masked. Though not before I saw it.

I stepped out of the truck ready to deal with whatever came next.

"What are those?" Dad asked, calmly. "That's not what I asked you to get."

"Yeah, I figured that out. Eventually," I answered, eyes down. "But not before they were all loaded. And then I didn't know what to do about it." I took a deep breath. Let it out slowly. Finally looking up at him, my lower lids filled again.

He sighed. "I can't use those. They have to go back."

My tears escaped.

"I can take them back if you need me to," he offered. His tone had softened, and at the same time, it was clear he expected the wood to be returned.

I knew he meant it. While his time could best be used at home, he was willing to save me from my morning blunder. I also knew that I would need to go back to Weiber's at some point in time, likely many times, in the next couple of years. It was still a possibility I'd actually die of embarrassment if I returned quickly, though. In the event I didn't actually expire from my own humiliation, however,

I'd be damned if I'd let Dad go back for me and let them all chuckle about my error at my expense. Not today—or any of the rest of the days to come.

I wiped my face. I squared my shoulders, readying myself for a large piece of humble pie. "Nope. I've got it."

"Do you know what you're getting this time?" he asked as I opened the truck door and perched on the edge of the seat, preparing to leave.

"Yes," I sighed. "I worked that out on the way home. We need eight twelve-foot 2x6s, right?" I shut the door and braced myself for my return to the lumber yard.

He smiled, a mixture of pity and pride on his face, "Yeah, that's it."

❄ ❄ ❄

Back at Wieber's, I parked, grabbed the receipt, and readied myself.

The bell rang above the door, and I walked toward the counter. Dale, who had checked me out twenty minutes ago, stood there. "What can I do for you?" His usual question, asked in a typical friendly manner with an atypical eyebrow raise, began what I feared would be a painful interaction. I willed the tears to stay in my head.

I handed him the receipt. "I need to return this order and get eight twelve-foot 2x6s instead," I explained slowly and with precision. "Please," I whispered, coming out both as a request and an apology.

My eyes looked down. My head repeated *Don't cry. Don't cry. Don't cry.*

He took the paper and set to work. He didn't say anything, and I wasn't about to look up to see his face.

After a brief moment, confident my tears would stay put, I stole a glance at him while he worked. I watched Dale writing down what seemed to be the same set of wood I was trying to return. Desperate to leave with the right order this time, I responded, hand up to stop him, "Wait, I don't want more of those!" I realized as I spoke, though, that he was trying to return my incorrect order first.

He looked up, just shy of annoyed.

"I'll just let you do your job," I said quietly, lowering my hand and looking to the ground again, hoping for a pit to open me up and swallow me whole. *Rest in peace, Cari, dead of shame.*

"Thank you. I will," he answered curtly. Yet his answer wasn't rude. As I stood there, I contemplated that there were any number of ways I could take his response, including but not limited to: He was going to deal with this silly girl professionally, but he was getting tired of her interfering with his work, which would have been done with less time and irritation had she gotten her numbers straight to start with. Or mentioned it was wrong before she left the first time. Or if Clare had shown up to fix the order instead. Or gotten it himself to start with. It slowly occurred to me that while all of those possibilities had merit, I might also be getting credit for owning up to my mistake, but only if I could keep my mouth shut until the transaction was rectified and complete. Even if I was incorrect, I was beginning to own the last thought for myself.

Mere minutes, or just shy of an eternity later, I was given a new paper receipt to show the worker outside.

I pulled the truck into the same spot where the beams had been loaded half an hour ago. I took a deep breath, released it slowly, and opened the window. "I'm back." I smiled. I handed the same worker the new receipt, one step closer to ending this unfortunate transaction. "Here you go. I need this instead. I'm sorry."

He took a look at the paper, seemingly not surprised to see me, and smiled back, "Just give me a few minutes, and you can be on your way." He unloaded the beams, also without undue commentary or complaint, and loaded the wood Dad actually wanted.

"Thank you," I smiled slightly and waved, both ready to leave the premises and to end this humbling event. I was pleasantly surprised at the lack of humiliating sneers and snide comments I'd had to endure, which surprisingly numbered zero. At least that I could hear. Evidently, everyone had been given strict instructions about customer service. Or, perhaps, each had hoped they weren't the one to make me cry.

As I drove away, the right order finally secured in the truck bed, I let out one more deep breath and shook my head at myself. I'd be back to Wieber's again in the future, but next time, I'd be sure to listen more carefully. In fact, maybe I would actually write the order down.

I was still alive, though. Embarrassed? Absolutely. Was today's lesson learned in the most painful way possible? You betcha. But it turned out that messing up, admitting it, and fixing it wasn't the end of the world after all. After today, I was growing confident in one thing—I could survive my own mistakes.

THREE SQUARE FEET AN HOUR

"Did you eat your high-powered Cheerios this morning? We have a roof to tear off," Dad smiled as he walked into the barn. Tear-offs were not my favorite, as I had a definite size and strength disadvantage to the guys on the crew. While my experience and dogged determination to do my fair share allowed me to hold my own, the first day of a new job left me not only just as filthy and smelly as everyone else, but also completely drained in my attempts to avoid being the weakest link. With the weather forecasting low to mid-nineties, my dread for the day ahead more than matched the level of my father's enthusiasm.

During our morning meeting, Dad briefed us on the new job and what he wanted done by the end of the day. We were working on a flat roof shaped like Oklahoma, a panhandle over a hallway that opened up to a big square roof over a screened-in porch. We would be tearing off the existing tar roof and putting down plywood in its place. He'd get us started; we'd then tear off the rest before lunch while he went to check out another prospective roof job. I would be in charge, adding yet another burden to what was already going to be a long day. We would put the roof back together in the afternoon. Dad's plan sounded simple. Easy. They always did.

We packed the truck. Our tool of choice for the day, a shingle spud, had a three-foot handle, grips on top, much like a snow shovel. The business end was a heavy metal attachment with a dozen sharp teeth across its 12" flat span. The teeth could be used to rip up shingles, but also fit well under existing cracks in order to create or enlarge holes in defective roofing material. Roofing nails also fit well between the teeth and could be removed by simply prying up with the handle. While meant for shingle roofs, they were equally effective in tearing apart any number of things. Today, we were going to use this tool to remove a leaking flat tar roof.

When we arrived at the job, everyone pulled a spud from the back of the work truck. Dad put the ladder up by the side of the house, and we climbed up to get a look at the roof. It was black and dirty, with a few cracks. Looking at it confirmed my suspicions that Dad's intentions for the day were a bit lofty, as the square part seemed much larger than his description.

The morning had been cool, and the shaded spot where Dad decided to start was perfect in every way—if the goal was to remove tar. It was both cold and the material old. While old tar is sometimes brittle, this particular spot was just thick enough that it wanted to stick together. It was attached to a piece of drip edge that had come loose from the roof itself, rusted nail dangling in the breeze, and had become one with the previously mentioned tar chunk. They were a team, emotionally attached to each other, desperate to cling to each other for eternity. Using a shingle spud, Dad put a metal tooth under the loosened drip edge, and with one gentle downward push of the handle, easily lifted the married pair. Dad smiled, "Just look at that. You'll be done by 10," his morning plan now on fast-forward with the ease of his first tear-off attempt. I scowled slightly, knowing that this shaded, easily accessible piece of tar was in no way a true indication of how the rest of the morning was going to go. It had been my experience over the years that the easier my father thought the tear-off was going to be, the less likely it was to meet his timeline.

With his hopes high and a quick check to make sure we had everything we needed, Dad turned to me. "I'll see you in a couple of hours. You'll probably have it all off, don't you think?"

"No," I sighed, "I don't. It's supposed to get up to the mid-nineties, and you started in the shade. The whole square part has been in the sun the whole morning already." I could see Tony rolling his eyes at me, accusing me of being melodramatic.

"Well," Dad responded slowly, humoring me, "I sharpened the spuds, so they're ready to go. Just plug along and do the best you can. I'll be back before lunch." He got on the ladder, stopping when his head was roof level. " We can get the sheeting on this afternoon," he added, making his goal known again before he sank out of sight.

I sighed again and turned to my crew. Tony had claimed a spot on the panhandle where Dad started, hoping that the ease of the first piece would continue for him. Jared, the only non-family member on the crew that morning, was looking for a good entry point that wouldn't interfere with Tony but would keep him in the shade for a bit longer. Roger, however, just stood there.

Turning, I found a crack near the end of the panhandle and set to work. I stuck a tooth into the crack and lifted slightly so the entry point would be a bit bigger. I pulled back the spud and thrust it forward into the same spot. It stopped quickly, the tar unchanged. My dad, of course, had found the one spot on the roof willing to have an amicable divorce. The rest would require brute force, curses, and perhaps alimony. I sighed.

I tried again, this time pulling the spud back a bit farther so it could gain more speed. I pushed it firmly toward my entry point. It stopped quickly. The tar, which was only an inch wide, had lifted less than half an inch and was still connected to the roof. I sighed again. I hated tear-offs. I hated tar.

I silently cursed the man who had created tar and tried yet again, this time pulling the spud back a bit farther yet, so it could gain more momentum. I pushed it firmly toward the piece of tar that now seemed to be taunting me. The spud stopped quickly. I, however, did not. My hand pulled off the handle as my body, not affected by the stubborn tar, continued in the direction I had aimed, and I slid to one knee. I quickly turned to see if anyone had witnessed my fall. The only observer seemed to be my spud, the handle of which had been stuck in the air. It fell to the roof slowly, laughing at me.

That's when I heard Roger, whose younger-brother-radar was on, chuckle from around the corner. "Get to work, Rog," I grumbled, losing what little patience I had. I stood up, shoulders stooped.

The sun, up for over two hours, had made this a picture-perfect summer morning, unless you were trying to tear off a roof. The black tar absorbed every warm ray sent its way, making it sticky and malleable. Had the tar been a bit thicker, the cool tar on the bottom would have remained solid and more easily removed. The heat, however, had already made its way to the decking, greatly diminishing the power of the spud. All of the tar was sticky and determined to remain in holy matrimony to the decking with zealot-like devotion. There would be no large pieces of roofing removed this morning, other than the one so quickly and easily lifted by my father.

Looking around, I realized that the rest of the crew was having as much luck as I was. Tony had gotten one more piece, half the size of Dad's, removed from the corner in the shade. Jared had started and stopped in a couple of places, given the evidence of a few inchworm-sized pieces in his vicinity. Roger seemed to have been just standing there for quite some time, contemplating, tar, marriage, or maybe nothing at all. Not only did I hate tear-offs, but I was going to be the one Dad talked to when it seemed we had gotten nothing done.

The morning wore on in much the same way for the three of us. Push, stick, and lift, leaving only a black little squiggle to show for my effort, frequently followed by a mumbled curse word. "Get to work, Rog!" I repeated, as I moved to a new location in the hopes that a new start would yield better results. I only found more of the same. Push, stick, lift, black sticky pebble left on the roof, taunting me by sticking to the soles of my shoes as I relocated.

Tony, the creative one of the bunch, tried various spud angles in the hopes of finding the magical method that would allow us to avoid the disappointed head shake of my father. Jared was flip-flopping between my method of consistency and Tony's variety throughout the morning. This was his first job, and I could tell he was becoming more concerned at our lack of progress, or perhaps my agitation, as the morning wore on. Only Roger, who had quickly become the bane of my existence, seemed unconcerned. His lack of effort led me to believe that he had decided he probably couldn't get fired, and if he did, perhaps that would be better anyway.

Pausing in his work, Jared asked me, "We aren't getting very far, are we?"

"No, we're not," I replied, frustrated at his comment on the obvious. "I knew this would happen. Dad's good at making it look easy and then leaving."

"How long do you think it'll take to finish? We're not even close," he observed.

We had all stopped what we were doing and looked around, feeling as though the roof were fighting with us—and winning. There were a few spots of decking showing, but not many. "Well, this spot is probably four square feet," I said, pointing to the section where I had been working. "You're standing in a spot, that's what, six square feet? There's another four-foot square section over by Tony, a few other smaller sections. Do you suppose that's about ten square feet where Dad had started?" I paused, doing the math in my head. "I think we have around twenty-four square feet; all we have to show for two hours' worth of work." I wiped the sweat off my forehead and began to plan the explanation I was going to give my father.

"Well, there are four of us," Jared added as Tony moved to join the conversation.

"That's only three square feet an hour *per person*," sighed Tony, finishing the calculations. "I don't want to do the rest of the math.

It's going to take us over a week to tear off this job."

Roger just shrugged, feeling no need to do any math while on summer vacation.

We took a collective sigh, got back to work, and waited for the inevitable.

❄   ❄   ❄

Dad arrived shortly before lunch as promised. He parked the truck in the driveway. At this point, I wasn't the only one dreading his reaction. "How's it going up there?" Dad yelled up, smiling, evidently happy with his morning's work.

"Awful!" I yelled back and turned away, not waiting for his response.

Simultaneously, we stopped working, took a look around again, and realized that the roof looked very much as Dad had left it three hours ago. There were a few pieces of decking showing through in the random places where we had hoped to find easy entry, and multiple small pieces of tar sitting about, the exception being the big piece Dad tore off before he left. It sat there on the side of the roof, mocking us. "Do you think he'll be mad?" newly-hired-Jared whispered to me as we watched Dad approach the side of the house.

I sighed and whispered back, "I guess we'll find out soon enough." We watched the ladder shimmy slightly as Dad ascended.

As his head became level with the rooftop, his eyes opened in surprise. Dad's shock at our lack of progress was evident. His mouth opened, stunned, and the expected response came blurting out, "What in the hell have you guys been doing the whole time?" His head began shaking slowly in disappointment.

I was instantly angry, and met him at the ladder, defending myself, "We've been working the whole time! I told you it would take longer than you thought. The only piece that came off in one chunk was the one you did first thing this morning." My volume increased as I built my case; my arms began to flail about wildly for added emphasis. "We tried everything. It's hot and the tar is just thin enough to be a big pain in the ass," throwing in a swear word to emphasize my point. "We did the math. We're averaging three square feet an hour *per person*! At this rate, it's going to take two weeks to get done what you thought we'd get done by lunch!" I crossed my arms, waiting for his response.

Dad, clearly frustrated by both our lack of progress and my yelling, reached for my spud. "Give me that," he said, and he stuck the spud on the roof where I left off.

Now, I had been in a similar situation before. Anytime I couldn't do something, as a last resort, I'd begrudgingly ask for help. Then Dad would try one time, with almost no effort, and complete the task easily. Every. Time. It was maddening. It was with this expectation, Dad adding insult to injury by completing what I couldn't, that I got ready to defend myself, and the rest of the crew, anew as he set to work.

He stuck a tooth under a spot in the tar that looked inviting and lifted slightly. He backed up the spud and rammed it into the spot. I could tell by the set of his shoulders and the smug look on his face that he fully expected to prove us all wrong. The spud stopped. Abruptly. There was a half-inch by half-inch square piece of tar sitting on top of the tooth, still connected to the roof.

I smiled.

"Garumph," Dad quietly said to himself and pulled the spud back a bit farther, this time ramming it again with more vigor. The tiny piece of tar, matching the others lying about, lifted from the roof deck. My smile grew.

"Well, you dog," Dad whispered to the tar piece, using his *This is frustrating* catch-phrase. Then he got serious. "Vroom, vroo-oom-oom," Dad revved like an engine in the way he did any time extra muscle was required to move something out of the way. He pulled the spud back and thrust it forward with the extra power of his verbal-turbo boost. It stuck. Just as our spuds had been sticking all morning.

I relaxed, the evidence speaking for me.

Dad stood up, smirking, finally admitting defeat. "Averaging three square feet an hour *per person*, huh? Good thing I bid this one on time and material. This bugger is stuck on here good."

I had spent the morning worried about Dad's reaction. There were so many things that were out of my control—the heat, the tar, even Roger. I felt as though I was dangling and stuck, much like that taunting piece of drip edge, blaming myself. For the first time in my memory, though, Dad couldn't fix the problem any better or faster than we could. If he couldn't do it, then perhaps it couldn't be done—at least not by lunch. I was vindicated. It wasn't my failure; it was just how this job was going to go. Turns out, some things take time. A lot of it. Especially when you're only working at a pace of three square feet an hour.

VALUE

During our morning meeting in the barn, Dad let us know it was supposed to be over ninety degrees that day, and, as usual, he had lots planned for us to get finished before lunch. He gave each of us our assignment for the morning. I would be in charge of the corners.

Dad used the Conklin flat roofing system. It was a latex-based system that had an embedded polyester fabric in the middle layer. The latex was painted or sprayed on, so the finished product was one piece, with no cracks to allow water in. The top layer was white, so the sun's rays were reflected, making it cooler. If the roof was connected to an adjoining building or another roof, metal flashing was used to make a smooth transition from the existing structure to the new roofing system.

We were past the messy stage of the roof, tearing off the existing tar and flashing. In the days prior, we had been able to screw down four-foot by eight-foot sheets of plywood, caulk the seams, and apply the primer. We had also embedded narrow fabric on the inner seams. The flashing to the adjoining roof had also been tacked in place. This particular day, we would be putting down the next layer and securing the outer edge. The other guys had started to spray the latex liquid with the pump, roll out the four-foot-wide strips of fabric, and embed them in the same liquid.

I, however, using only a brush and a small can of latex paint, had been embedding a narrow roll of the same fabric into the second layer along the wall of the adjoining roof, along the edge of the flashing, and into the corners. I had to be careful of wrinkles and spacing as well in my dealings with all of the angles and edges. The job was both tedious and time-consuming. The guys had been covering hundreds of square feet in the first couple of hours. I, the lone female, had covered approximately ten square feet. Total. Maybe. I was on track to spend the entire morning on this one task. If judged only by quantity, I had been the least productive worker that day, by far.

The challenge of a wrinkle-free final product was compounded by the fact that Dad believed one brush should make it through an entire summer of work. This was problematic. To begin with, the latex coating, much thicker than paint, widened each of the bristles, especially the spot connecting the bristles to the handle, causing the entire brush portion to expand like a middle-aged waistline. Also, the brush was placed bristle side down in a can of water each day. Prior to the next use, the brush was pulled out of its pool. After a quick wire brushing and a firm shaking meant to get the worst of the dried gunk off the bristles, the battered brush was deemed fit for its next job. As it was midsummer, my aging tool for the day's task was less than ideal.

I gathered up my tools and headed back to work. I reminded myself not to be jealous of the boys with their smooth, large rollers and long straight paths. I knew their job took little brainpower. My job, on the other hand, required knowledge, skill, and patience. I appreciated the responsibility of the task, making sure the edge was sealed from leaks and there were no wrinkles to be found. While I enjoyed the challenge, I was also aware that it would look like I had accomplished very little at the end of the day.

I got to work in the fairly clean corner. I brushed away the last of the small tar pieces left from the day before and applied the initial coat of latex. I carefully placed the fabric just a bit higher than needed, as I knew from past experience I would eventually push a bunch of fabric into the corner. The extra would ensure I still had embedded fabric all the way under the cap, a very important piece connecting the two roofs. This roof was in town and shared a wall with the adjoining building, which went about eighteen inches higher than the surface of the roof. The tin cap covered the wall, ensuring not only that there were no leaks on this roof but also preventing leaks on the neighboring one, provided the taping on the flashing was done well. I needed to be careful to satisfy Dad's inspection.

I carefully applied the topcoat, fabric settling into the corner. Just as I predicted, my swollen brush moved the way I wanted it to, despite its mid-summer girth. I unrolled more of the fabric and moved along the outer edge of the flashing. I proceeded down the length of the wall, making sure to keep the fabric straight and my work wrinkle-free.

A few yards later and with the weather growing ten degrees warmer, my slow work halted entirely. I realized the chimney, coming out of the roof, was also connected to the wall. To add to the complexity, part of the cap was cut away to allow it to rise above the roof. Corners and edges everywhere. Instead of dealing with just the roof and its flashing, I also had to worry about the flashing on the chimney, the other roof, and two additional corners, all of which were going to interfere with each other. I paused to make a game plan.

The boys rolled out another ten feet.

I problem-solved, realizing I would have to start with all of the seams at the bottom and work my way up. "Think like a drip" was one of our roofing mantras. The top seams would need to overlap those on the bottom, preventing drips from sneaking under any seams.

I had no intention of allowing any drips to make their way into the building.

I placed my brush in the shade to prevent the latex from drying any faster than necessary and executed my strategy. I set about cutting pieces to size, allowing extra lengths to push into and around corners. I knew this area was the most likely to leak. I also knew I would need to slowly take this one step at a time, completing each section carefully. Past experience had taught me how mistakes made for timely corrections—if I messed up step four, I frequently had to go back to step one.

The boys rolled on.

My plan made and tools in place, I set to work. Once all of the pieces had been laid out, I picked up the getting-gooey brush and set to work. The warming roof and my unexpected planning time had allowed the liquid latex to set, gel-like, on the brush. My first strokes were long and firm, intentionally pulling the latex toward the end of the bristles. All the lingering stickiness in the brush would pull at the fabric, creating unwanted air pockets and wrinkles, resulting in frustration and swearing.

Due in large part to the heat, it was as tricky as I had feared. The first piece went into the corner smoothly to start, but the heat caused the latex to get sticky quickly. This left wrinkles in the corner when there was too much product. When I tried to wipe away the excess, the fabric pulled out, creating an air pocket. Several deep breaths, some dirty fingers, and another firm brush cleaning later, the lower corners were finally complete and smooth.

The boys rolled on.

I cleaned out the brush again and set to work, determined to seal the seams running up and down.

Not long afterwards, Dad came up the ladder on the far side of the roof, the owner following behind. Dad was explaining today's portion of the roofing process, pointing at various things as they slowly meandered toward the center of the roof, making it possible for me to hear their discussion. "She is great at the details. I mean, she's really good," I overheard him talking about me, the only "she" on the roof that day.

Dad had always said to the crew, "The beauty of this system is in the details. Anyone can learn how to do it, but it takes a bit more to do it well." I continued to eavesdrop on the conversation. Dad didn't know I was listening, and I'm quite certain he didn't know what I really heard. As he continued to discuss my work, beneath his words, I heard: *She makes this system work. She does it well. She is competent.*

I think I always knew Dad brought us along because he could interact with his children, but I don't think I realized, until that moment, the significance of my contribution to the family business. It reinforced my belief that I had a great responsibility as a worker for our family, but it was the first time I remember comprehending the *worth* of my work. I had never truly understood until I overheard Dad's statement just how much I had to offer. My work was real. It was good. I, the roofer's daughter, had great value.

OFF THE ROOF:

LESSONS AS A WIFE

DUST BUNNY REBELLION

"Quash," my husband, Jay, repeated as he walked by with the folded laundry.

"It's obviously 'quell.' While your word choice might work, you're just annoyed that my word is better," I replied.

"Quash," he repeated, a bit louder, from our bedroom.

I sighed. "You're not right! The rebellion needs to be quelled," I responded, also a bit louder, as I scrubbed the dishes with a bit more vigor, annoyed that he wouldn't just agree with me.

We were cleaning the house on a rare Saturday morning to ourselves. Our new-to-us rental was much larger than either of our previous ones. The house was originally built for a large family. On top of the normal kitchen, living room, and dining room, there were four bedrooms and two and a half baths. In addition, there was also an office, a laundry room, and a sitting room, which contained only my childhood piano because, as newlyweds, we did not own enough furniture for all of the rooms. It was substantially more room than two people needed—or could clean with the regularity the space required.

Not only was the sheer space an issue, but so was time. I had just started my first full-time teaching job, which probably would have been enough to keep me busy. However, I was also the new varsity cross country coach, in large part because I was young, energetic, and the only applicant. My after-school time was spent at practice, as well as at least one race in the evening during the week and many Saturday invitationals. Jay was also working full-time and coming to several practices a week and all of the races as an assistant coach.

Needless to say, the housework had gotten away from us.

That morning, while looking for dirty laundry under the bed, I found a collection of dust bunnies. I believe I previously thought people just made up that term, but there they were. Several tufts of dust, slightly rounded, sitting by each other. Not full-grown rabbits, of course, but perhaps a nest of baby bunnies waiting patiently for their mother to return.

"Jay, we've really got to do better at cleaning. Have you looked under the bed lately? I found a collection of dust bunnies," I yelled, making sure he could hear the announcement of my discovery.

"Why would I look under the bed?" he yelled back from the other room. "It's like you're looking for more work to do. Can't we just stick to your already lengthy list of chores today?"

I looked again to make sure they were still there. "I'm definitely not looking for more work. But now that I've found them, I know they exist. And we need to do something about it."

"We?" he scoffed. "As in the 'royal we,' where you just added the task to my list?"

"Perhaps. That's actually a great idea," I smirked. "Look, there is a *collection* of dust bunnies. It's not like there's just one light little layer of dust. There are *tufts*, like baby bunnies. Come look at them."

"I'm not looking."

"If we don't do something about it, they'll grow into full-sized bunnies. Then what?" I reached beneath the bed and poked at one with my finger.

Realizing I was not going to let this go, he walked in and sighed, "What? Are you afraid they will attack us in our sleep? Like a dust bunny rebellion?" He stopped to see if I was seriously going to keep talking about the dust, only visible if you looked for it, under our bed.

I absolutely was.

I turned to face him. "Yes! A dust bunny rebellion! How will you be able to sleep tonight if it's not taken care of?" I smiled, daring him to back down from this issue that was quickly becoming a top priority.

"You want me to stop what I'm doing to quash a dust bunny rebellion?" He raised his eyebrow at me in disbelief.

I stood up and grabbed a dirty shirt off the pile yet to be washed on the floor. "No," I smirked, "I want you to add it to your list, per your suggestion." I flicked his backside with the shirt, playfully. "And I think you mean 'quell.'"

He grabbed my wrist and pulled me close, "I think if you want it done, it should get added to *your* list. And I mean what I said; the rebellion should be quashed," and he kissed my nose.

I chuckled. My husband was well-read, so I didn't usually win—or provoke—an argument involving word choice, but I was feeling confident in my pick. "It's definitely quell, Babe." I gathered up the rest of the laundry.

"Quash," he repeated confidently, leaving the bedroom like the matter was over.

"No, really," I followed, "it's quell. You know that. I mean, quash could work, but quell is obviously the better choice in this instance."

"Quash," he repeated, continuing to leave the room and the discussion.

I threw the laundry in the washing machine and started it. I then grabbed the cleaning supplies from the closet and headed to the bathroom. *I should let it go.* I thought to myself, while suspecting it was highly unlikely.

I finished cleaning the toilet, finding myself annoyed at the confidence in his less-than-perfect word choice. He could do better. And I could help him see the error in his ways. A playful war of wit was not so easily won in the Smith household, and we were, despite the very real irritation of having to clean and tidy, having fun with our continued back-and-forth. I finished packing up the cleaning supplies and headed into the office, where he was organizing the pile of mail that had accumulated, armed with new ammunition.

"Let's see what the Oxford Dictionary has to say," I returned to the discussion, dropped the supplies, and found what I was looking for on our bookshelf.

"We own a dictionary?"

"Yeah, someone gave it to us as a wedding present."

"Of course they did."

Admittedly, I found it a bit of an odd gift at the time. It seemed the giver may have known us and our upcoming marital issues better than we knew ourselves. I turned to the section labeled Q and readied myself to let the dictionary settle the matter once and for all. I read the definitions aloud.

Quash /kwosh/ v.tr. 1. annul; reject as not valid, esp. by a legal procedure. 2. suppress; crush (a rebellion, etc.).

Quell /kewl/ v. tr. 1. a) a crush or put down (a rebellion, etc.) b) reduce (rebels, etc.) to submission. 2. suppress or alleviate

The answer, to me, was clear. Well, at least it wasn't an obvious loss. Not only was I not completely wrong, but it could be argued I was *more* right, which was becoming a bigger deal by the minute.

"See, I'm right," Jay pronounced. He folded his hands on the desk and leaned forward, daring me to continue.

And continue I did. "Ah, no. I'm obviously *more* right. It's true, both words contain a definition about crushing a rebellion, but mine also refers to *reducing rebels*. And our dust bunnies look like they are preparing to attack. We need to *alleviate* this problem."

He sat back in the chair. Silent. The smirk on his face, which I had witnessed before, communicated an unstated victory and unwillingness to budge from his stance. It seemed my new husband was not going to back down from this argument. He wanted to be right as much as I did.

How unfortunate—for both of us.

I sighed, put the dictionary back, and left to do another chore.

As the organization and cleaning of the day continued, a periodic "Quell" from me and "Quash" response from him could be heard, our lively banter and laughter persisting. The house looked better, but the dust bunnies remained—as did our control issues, collecting and resurfacing, frequently throughout our marriage. Though we thought we knew each other well before we said our wedding vows due to our eight-year courtship, it seemed we had much to learn about each other.

While it could be argued that both of us had equally correct words, I eventually learned that we needed to work on meeting in the middle, finding a way to positively compromise while keeping our sense of humor. Perhaps our dust bunnies didn't need to be quashed or quelled as much as they needed to be managed in a positive and productive way.

SOUP ON SUNDAYS

It was Sunday. We were having chicken soup with hot dogs with my parents after church. While this meal may seem like an unusual Sunday dinner to most, it holds a special place in my heart because it was the one we always had at Grandma's house when I was little. As an adult, I found myself getting up—again—that time to slice more bread. I had already gotten up to get a butter knife. Then I had to get up again after my first couple of bites to get the carafe of coffee. Had it been any meal other than Sunday breakfast, I would have been annoyed, yelling, "Get it yourself!" to anyone daring to ask me to leave my seat once more. I smiled, though, enjoying the scene before me so much I didn't mind the interruptions.

✻ ✻ ✻

The door opened, and her face filled the space, smiling. I smiled back. "Oh, it's so good to see you!" she said as she opened the door wide, let me in, and reached to give me a hug. Her short strawberry-colored curls tickled my nose as she whispered in my ear, "I've been thinking about you all week," while she embraced me entirely. I believed her wholeheartedly.

I was cherished.

I hugged her back, tightly, taking in the smell of fresh bread and chicken surrounding her. She pulled away to get a good look at me.

I was seen.

"Thank you for coming. What should we have for breakfast today?" she asked.

I was loved.

It was the beginning of another Sunday brunch with Grandma K. My brothers piled in and received their hugs and welcome, while I hung up my coat and took off my shoes. The boys quickly headed to the toy room and Dad to the recliner in the living room. She asked, "What are you hungry for today? Does soup sound good?" Soup always sounded good. It was also what we had every time. Soup and hot dogs, though I wouldn't know it was an unlikely pairing for another ten years, was my favorite meal at Grandma's.

I responded, "That sounds great to me. What do you need me to do?" I knew the answer already. I was the Hot Dog Counter.

"Why don't you find out how many hot dogs everyone wants?" she offered, then she moved into the kitchen with Mom.

I dutifully found Dad and each of my brothers to ask how many hot dogs each person wanted. The number was always the same, as was Grandma's reaction when I told her the final tally. "Oh, that can't be enough," she scoffed. "Why don't you add a couple more? We don't want to run out." I knew Grandma considered running out of food a very serious offense. I did as I was told, opening the packages and placing the counted hot dogs in the boiling water, knowing there would be a couple of hot dogs left at the end of the meal. Someone (usually Dad) would have to eat more than they ordered—because Grandma said so.

Mom and Grandma continued assembling the soup. I watched this exchange play out while I got out the bread and put it on a plate, one side of whole wheat and one side of white. The soup started with broth and rice, then the celery and onions were added. None of these ingredients were measured; Grandma knew exactly how much to use. I got the ketchup, mustard, and pickles out of the fridge. There was always a small piece of leftover chicken in there waiting to be added to the pot. It was a quiet process, Mom and Grandma moving, choreographed, working together. I wondered, though never voiced, my confusion as a can of Campbell's chicken noodle soup got added to the pot of Grandma's homemade chicken noodle soup. I set the table. There was the inevitable taste-testing as the egg noodles and seasonings were added. "What do you think this needs?" Grandma asked Mom, which frequently ended in a decision to add another sprinkling of celery salt.

"Call your dad and brothers," Mom directed me, while moving the soup to the table.

Grandma took inventory. "Oh, I cut some carrots. Let's not forget those," she said, moving toward the refrigerator. "And the jelly. We can't forget the jelly." I wondered at the odd condiment addition but left to announce lunch to the others. As I left the kitchen, I heard, "And be sure to grab another chair!"

A ruckus roared as my brothers ran into the kitchen, at various speeds, taking their place at the table. My dad took the long way around, finding the dessert plate already assembled on the far counter and taking a sample. "Oh, Clare," Grandma reprimanded, in a tone much like the one my mother used on my brothers, "that's for later."

Mom swatted at his hand, exclaiming, "Why don't you sit down?" while he smiled, shrugged, and continued to chew. My brothers smiled at Dad getting into trouble as we all settled in.

Grandma was the last one to sit, grabbing the butter still on the counter.

"Ok, let's pray." Dad clapped his hands together impatiently.

We said the final Amen, completed the Sign of the Cross (with varying degrees of precision by my brothers), and dug in. Mom ladled soup for the boys, who were all handing her their bowls at the same time from their various places at the table. "Oh, take some of the thick stuff," Grandma instructed Mom as she ladled. I took care of myself, so I got a piece of bread and started buttering it. Dad munched on a pickle, waiting his turn. Grandma left the table again.

Things quieted down as the boys began to eat instead of talk, and Grandma returned with some coffee. I watched her sit again as I took a bite of hot dog loosely rolled in a piece of whole wheat bread, covered in only mustard. With everyone seated and eating, she finally filled her own bowl with soup and got a hot dog out of the pot. "Oh, my. I'll get some more bread," she exclaimed, though the bread plate was not empty. She got up again. I watched her as I ate another spoonful of soup.

By the time Grandma sat again, her bowl of soup was no longer steaming. Almost everyone else was on their second helping.

She peered into the half-full pot. "Oh my, are you sure you've had enough? And look at all those hot dogs." She tisked and looked at my brother. "Is that all you're going to eat? Don't you want another hot dog?" He shrugged and continued eating the one in his hand, unsure of the correct response.

"Ma, sit down," Dad sort of told and sort of asked her.

"I just want to make sure there's enough," she said again, smiling. "Will you please pass the ketchup?"

Grandma's adult soup bowls had a wide lip around the basin decorated with flowers, vines, and gold. It was on this edge that she placed a big dollop of ketchup, dipped her large spoon in it, scooped up the soup, and ate it. She beamed as if she were enjoying a fine delicacy, while I shuddered and tried not to throw up in my mouth.

"There are more hot dogs if you want more," she said as she peered at the extras floating in the pot. "Though, I suppose you boys want some dessert." Her eyes twinkled, as did theirs.

She got up yet again to grab the plate containing both cookies and pieces of chocolate cake.

❄   ❄   ❄

I smiled, recalling the memory, as I returned with the coffee. "You want some more, Dad? Mom? There's still a bit left." I filled our cups and sat again. I've gotten up at least three times. My soup, while not cold, was no longer steaming. I smiled, finding I didn't mind.

My boys grew quiet, eating their soup and asking for more bread. Were it Thursday, I'd tell them to get their own, but it was

Sunday. I got up one more time to get the plate on the counter, brownies and cookies ready—minus the bite taken earlier from Tristan.

Putting the bread on the table, I paused to take in the moment—remember it. My memories of soup on Sunday, both old and new, filled my heart.

I loved them—the people around the table and the woman in my heart.

Cherished. Seen. Loved—tasting like a bowl of chicken soup on Sunday.

TIMING

"Could you find out some dates for our fall camping trip from your friends at work today? I'd like to get it on the calendar," I asked while finishing up my shower.

"Kevin will be out of the office today," he responded as he finished drying himself off.

I smirked. "Too bad we don't live in a time when you can contact your friends if they're out of the office." I smiled at my witty response, "I guess it will just have to wait." I finished rinsing my hair and opened the curtain to see my husband, wrapped in a towel, just about ready to leave the bathroom. Our hand towel, used to catch the water from his very hairy body as he dried off, was saturated except for the corners. The towel I had gotten out of the cupboard before I stepped into the shower was nowhere to be seen, however. "Where's my towel?" I demanded.

His eyebrow lifted. "Hmm?" was his guttural response. He walked away, the door still open.

I could see it.

Evidently, he kicked my towel out of the bathroom, and it slid across the wood floor of our dining room. It lay ten feet away, partially beneath the hutch. I stood in the shower, dripping, and realized the summer morning was cooler than I thought. I shut the curtain.

I sighed. "Kaedyn!" I yelled at our youngest, currently taking advantage of morning screen time in the living room. "Will you please get my towel? It's under the hutch."

Nothing. No response at all.

"Kaedyn!" I tried a bit louder. "The towel!"

"I no canna find it!" he yelled back.

"That's because you aren't even looking!" I wasn't going to die of hypothermia, but it was getting downright cold. "Get in here, please. I need your help."

I could hear him sigh like his mother and pause his game. He walked into the bathroom. He saw my head peeking out of the curtain and looked at the ground, seeing the soggy hand towel. "It's wight there!" he pointed, exasperated at my obvious lack of intelligence. Job complete, he turned to walk away.

"No! That one is all wet and *way* too small," my tone of voice matching his. "The one by the hutch. The big dry one."

He turned to look. "I don see it."

I swallowed a sigh. I needed his help. "Look at the hutch." He turned around. "Now look down."

"Oh," his head turned; he smiled. I couldn't help but smile back. "I get it."

"Thank you," I said as he handed it back to me and rushed back to his game. I promptly shut the door and began toweling off. *I'm sure Jay thinks he's funny*. I thought to myself as I dried off and warmed up. And he was indeed funny, but there was no need to let him know his response was almost as entertaining as my initial comment. I wrapped myself in the towel.

He walked back in, now dressed, still smiling, and blocking the doorway. I punched him in the belly. "That wasn't very nice," I said, standing nose to chin with him.

"You're right. Your comment wasn't very nice, and neither was that punch," he said and kissed my nose. He moved to finish getting ready while I relayed the story of my struggles in getting a dry towel. By the end of my tale, he was laughing. I laughed, too.

"Sounds to me like you need to be nicer to your husband," he concluded, pointing out the day's obvious lesson. "Why don't you write about that?"

"Oh, I just might," I retorted. "But you've got it all wrong. I don't have to work on being nice, I just have to work on my timing."

THE INSURANCE BILL

Growing up, there was a change in my mother every three months. Her shoulders grew closer to her ears, the shape of her mouth flattened as her smile flatlined, and a negative cloud, which I couldn't name at the time, seemed to descend around her. My parents didn't talk about money problems around us. Dad said, later in my life, "Money issues shouldn't be talked about around kids. They don't need to worry about things like that." It was the related questions, "When do you want me to send that check? From what account? Did you call Mr. Thelen last night about that bill?" that Mom asked, an unnatural tightness in her voice, which let me know something worrisome was going on.

With Dad being a self-employed roofer and Mom a stay-at-home mother, we lived beneath the government-declared poverty line. Dad would frequently say, while shaking his head in disbelief, "The government says we're poor, but we have it so good." I don't think I was consciously aware of money issues in my family growing up, but I believe I was unconsciously aware that money was a frequent worry of my mother's, especially when the insurance bill was due.

Dad usually seemed to wave off these questions with less concern than I believe Mom thought he should. "We need to have faith that the Lord will provide," seemed to be the source of his trust as the due date of the insurance bill loomed ever closer. Mom's practical side—the one which saw the bills and the bank account whose number wasn't big enough to cover them—I believe, spoke up during her own prayers, questioning just exactly how did the Good Lord expect her to make out a check and send it when the money to back it wasn't there.

In a lot of ways, Dad was right about the quality of our life. We ate well—both in quality and quantity. Mom worked hard to feed our family of seven. We had a big garden out back, which Mom tended and then canned the bounty of every year. We bought beef, at cost, from the happy cows down the road on my uncle's farm that grazed on grass. We ate organically before it was the buzzword of the media.

Mom's skills in the kitchen were impressive. Not only did she make wonderful homemade whole-wheat bread, homemade pies, jams, and jellies, but she also had the miraculous ability to make a mostly empty cupboard into a meal fit for kings. A turkey carcass became stock, pieces of leftover meat and veggies became soup, rice, and a can of Campbell's Cream of Celery soup was transformed into a casserole. Very few things were processed, as pop and potato chips were for special occasions only. I remember there was even enough for everyone to have seconds if they wanted. The rule was "Take all you want, but eat all you take." Nothing was ever wasted, but no one left the table hungry.

Not only did Mom have the magic to stretch a dollar in the kitchen, there were a number of other things she did to make ends meet in our one-income family. We purchased much of our clothing at garage sales and consignment shops, looking carefully for stains or loose seams before purchasing. Most of the Christmas gifts were very practical and always had a use—shoes for an upcoming sporting season, a warm coat, even underwear. There was rarely enough money or time in the summer to go away for a whole week on vacation, but we would splurge on one-day outings to museums and amusement parks. We would pack a special lunch of bologna sandwiches, fruit, Faygo pop, and potato chips. The salty, crunchy treat always brought a smile to my face and let me know the day was really special.

I didn't feel deprived or want for things I didn't have growing up. I knew that my parents were doing the best they could for us. I also had friends who lived in much the same way, so it seemed normal—just how people lived. Our basic needs were always met. We didn't always have everything we wanted, but we had what we needed. We were really quite happy, as we had each other and life was good.

"Appreciate what you have" and "Frugal living can be wonderful" were the messages of my childhood. However, there were several other unintended lessons learned when the insurance bill was due, which I also carry with me. Mom cleaned, saved, and reused bread bags and Ziploc bags to hold green beans from the garden or leftover strawberry shortcake rolls. The old coffee grounds would stay in the coffee maker and new ones would be added so coffee wouldn't have to be purchased as often. Also, I found it disturbing that Mom had a number of things in her closet that were more than ten years old—a faded pair of jeans, a well-used pair of sandals, and the only winter coat I'd ever known her to wear. "Who would want to wear the same thing for so long?" my young mind wondered.

At some point in my childhood, though I don't remember the moment, I started to realize that some of my mother's odd household practices weren't chosen so much as were necessary to make ends meet. Having a garden and canning was a lot of work. Reusing a bag was practical. Coffee didn't taste much different from recycled coffee grounds. Perhaps, though, there were times when my mom would have loved to buy a new dress or pair of shoes. There were times when Mom didn't want to make dinner from scratch, again. By the time the insurance bill came and was paid for, though, there wasn't anything left for those wanted, yet unnecessary items. It required sacrifices to make ends meet. While my father was celebrating our lack of money, I realized not everything about financial concerns was wonderful.

As an adult, I am part of a two-income household where having enough money to feed my children really isn't an issue. There are a number of things I have carried over from the frugal beginnings of my childhood, however. I tend a garden because the vegetables taste really good, it gets us outside, and it's cheap. Leftovers frequently morph into another meal, as we love a good casserole. We eat venison and raise chickens because we believe they taste better than what you can buy in the store. I also want my kids to know where food comes from. My kids know I consider potato chips a special treat. There is a focus on healthy eating in our house.

Also, I've been known to buy some of my children's clothing at consignment shops, because they're barely worn and much cheaper. I now own a few articles of clothing, like my favorite pair of jeans, which I've had for more than ten years, because they fit just right and are really comfortable. I am able to choose which of these childhood practices my family maintains, however. While perhaps not always required, doing some of the things my parents did out of necessity growing up has allowed my family to spend that money on other things we really enjoy. We have owned several different cars, have a big screen TV, and own a number of technological gadgets because we want them—even if we don't need them.

Despite all of the wonderful things I carry with me from my childhood, there is one unspoken fear that haunts me. Every once in a while, despite its illogical presence, the tension and anxiety of having enough to make ends meet lingers in the back of my mind. It creeps up, unexpectedly, as our bank account gets close to zero at the end of the pay period. Despite the rational conversations my husband and I have about our investments, pensions, and IRAs, as the account number dwindles down ever closer to zero, it causes my shoulders to grow closer to my ears, the shape of my mouth to flatten as my smile flatlines, and a negative cloud, which I can now identify, to descend around me. Even though my brain tells me we are going to be fine, my heart remembers the worry in our house when the insurance bill was due. I still reuse Ziploc bags.

STREP THROAT

G rowing up, I was a strep throat magnet. I seemed to have caught it multiple times each winter. One particularly bad season, the doctor said that if I got it one more time, they were going to take my tonsils out. Hoping that sheer will would prevent me from surgery, I decided not to get it again. I'm not sure if desire had anything to do with it, but I still have my tonsils.

Strep always started as a little tickle in the back of my throat. I would pretend it wasn't there while also noticing the back of my throat close in, and my glands swell slowly and with purpose. I would chew my food into mush and then carefully swallow, so Mom wouldn't know. In hindsight, I'm sure that was a dead give-away, as no one chewed carefully with seven mouths at the table—seconds were only an option if the first helping was swallowed in large chunks. I may have been the only girl in the family, but I knew how to get my fair share.

"Do you have a sore throat?" she would ask after dinner.

"I'm fine," I would mutter and quickly escape without making eye contact.

Eventually, my throat would swell to the point where even spit was hard to swallow. Denial of my illness became harder at this point, but I would push on with as much vigor as I could muster in my weakened state. I was aware of the tight financial situation in the house and knew a trip to the doctor's office wasn't in the budget. I would need a prescription filled, costing more. I didn't want to be a burden, make it more difficult to make ends meet, or make my parents go without something they wanted or, worse, needed. If I could pretend that my sore throat would go away for just one more day, perhaps my body would comply with what my mind so desperately wanted to believe. I wished this despite all of the evidence, in the form of excessive saliva, to the contrary.

"Do you have a sore throat?" Mom would ask after my evening snack lay uneaten—an unheard of occurrence unless something was amiss.

"Yeah, it hurts a little," I lied, denial giving way to the reality that a doctor's visit was inevitable. I lay on the couch. The chills that had started moments before were attacking my body with a vengeance now that the truth was out, and I no longer needed to pretend. Mom would go into the kitchen, brew some slippery elm tea, and make plans to rearrange her schedule the next day to get me in to the doctor's. I bundled up under a blanket, and the boys were told to leave me alone.

"Drink it while it's hot," Mom would say every time as she handed me the cup. I sipped my tea as directed, though, at this point in my illness, my throat continued to close no matter how hot or cool it became. Swallowing was agony, and the minutes crawled on as I cursed myself for waiting so long and felt a bit guilty that I wasn't strong enough to fight it off this time.

I would lie in misery that night, spitting into a Kleenex, as all hope of swallowing was gone with my acceptance that strep throat had taken up residence. I was left weak and waiting until morning.

The doctor's visit was always the same, with the only change being the number of brothers who were dragged along. An antiseptic smell accosted us in the waiting room while Mom filled out paperwork. Guilt tugged at me, as I knew the cost of being here was not in the budget. Once we were brought to the exam room, I would sit, miserable, while the nurse took my vital signs. I would sit quietly and hear the ever-so-slight *tisk* in the back of her throat when she saw how swollen my tonsils had gotten. Another wave of guilt attacked me for waiting so long, letting it get so bad. The doctor would enter, take one look, and mention strep, as if we all didn't know what it was, and then take a painful, choking culture. We would wait. The nurse would come back to confirm what we all knew and hand out a prescription.

We would go to the pharmacy in St. Johns. I was punched in the gut by guilt, again, as I knew my parents would have to spend more money. Feelings of relief followed quickly, though, as I knew the medicine would kick in soon. I would feel better by dinner and be able to swallow breakfast. The event always left me feeling a bit battered—by both the bacteria and my emotions. I vowed to be stronger next time.

One night, as an adult, I went to bed ignoring the sting in my throat the way I did when I was a child. When I woke up the next morning, after finally acknowledging that I had a sore throat, I found myself continuing to believe it wasn't that bad. I realized, though, I was no longer a little girl. It was ok to miss work, even and especially when I was sick. No one wanted the sick girl to be at work. I no longer had to hide my sore throat from my mother. My husband and I had health insurance and could handle the copay for the office visit. I had a job that allowed for paid sick days, so I would not see a difference in my paycheck. I was no longer eight years old. It wasn't going to be a financial burden for me to be sick. It was ok for me not to be at work.

When the chills started in the shower, I accepted the fact that I had strep throat. The body aches and headache settled in as I got dressed and called into work. I made sub plans, brewed myself a cup of hot slippery elm tea, and prepared to go to the doctor's office. A quick visit confirmed my suspicions. I went to St. Johns and happily paid the $10 copay for my antibiotic, knowing I would soon be well. It felt good to look forward to sitting on the couch, binge-watching a show. For the first time in my life, I was able to admit to myself that I wasn't being weak—I was just sick. And that's ok. I will feel better tomorrow.

DWELLING

My Grandma K lost her first child during childbirth. No one really talked about it. The only statement, heard multiple times, was, "She didn't dwell on it," and the topic of conversation changed quickly. Not finding that a very complete answer to what I considered a difficult life event to deal with, I pursued the matter. I hinted around, asking about the circumstances with my aunts, who gave me similar answers. I even made it a point to stop at my grandmother's sister's house to try to get more information. My great aunt, eight years younger than my grandmother, had had more than her fair share of heartache as well, losing two husbands and a child over the course of her life. "Oh, she didn't dwell on it. Those things happen," she matter-of-factly stated. So convincing was her tone that I was led to believe she thought "not dwelling" was perhaps the best way that the situation could, or should, have been handled.

I spent years wondering about this cryptic message, repeated by the women in my life, as the way to deal with life's hardships and heartaches.

❊   ❊   ❊

It was exactly 3:07 a.m., and my husband woke me up. "I need to go to the hospital," he said breathlessly. "I'm not doing well." He spoke with both fear and desperation.

He hadn't been doing well for a couple of weeks. He had been struggling with anxiety, again. The new medicine he had been trying wasn't working as well as we'd hoped. Things had finally come to a head.

"I'm taking you in," I responded, instantly awake, registering that we were now in uncharted territory with his anxiety just by the sound of his voice. I quickly got dressed while considering which person I could wake up in the middle of the night to watch the kids, and what I was going to do about work tomorrow, only a few short hours away.

Jay, meanwhile, was pacing and breathing in short gasps, unable to catch his breath. His heart raced, almost visibly, as he struggled to calm down. I struggled with the desire to leave immediately, as his full-blown panic attack continued to ratchet up. I stood by, knowing there was nothing I could do to make it better. My helplessness was made worse by the thought of not being able to get him help right away, as our boys lay sleeping, unaware of what was amiss, and I had yet to make a phone call to someone to come stay with the kids.

My first choice for childcare was my friend, a nurse, who I knew was working that night and wasn't available. I did not want to call my parents, but my options for people who lived close by were limited. Jay had gone outside, hoping to get in the car and on our way quickly, but began pacing the driveway instead, his hands shaking at his sides. I stood on the porch dialing my parents' number and hoping for the best. The phone rang four times before my dad picked it up. "Hello?" was his groggy response.

"Hi, Dad. It's Cari. Jay has been struggling with anxiety lately and isn't doing well tonight. Can someone come over to watch the kids so I can take him to the hospital?" I heard a muffled response on the other end as he talked to my mother. I heard her response, no words, only her higher-pitched voice, on the other end. I waited. They continued to talk on the other end, but their voices were distant. I began to wonder if my father had put down the phone as their discussion continued. I waited. There was no response. Jay looked at me with his eyebrows raised, non-verbally asking if we would be able to leave soon. I shrugged, still waiting, still helpless.

It soon became apparent that Dad had indeed put the phone down. I disconnected the conversation on my end and called back. There was a busy signal. I knew Mom and Dad's landline had call waiting, which meant the phone had not been turned off. I could picture it lying quietly on its side on their dresser, green light still on. Their cell phones were never on. I sighed. Jay paced, hands still shaking, beginning to look like a drug user in withdrawal. I tried to phone again. The incessant beeping continued, like a clock ticking, only with more urgency. My husband continued to walk the edge of the driveway. I attempted to call four more times, not expecting a different response so much as wanting to *do* something. I stood calmly on the porch. Inside, however, the fear that I was abandoned by my parents competed with the feeling of being torn between wanting to help my husband and to protect my children. I was forced to watch more pacing.

I saw a set of headlights in the distance, and I prayed that my mother, in her attempt to get out the door quickly, had just forgotten to hang up the phone. The rumble of the tires became much too loud to be their Chrysler Pacifica. As the lights came closer, a semi barreled by.

Three minutes crawled past before another set of headlights popped up in the distance. I hoped for rescue, despite the fear moving ever more definitively into my stomach. The lights came and passed. Fear took up permanent residence as I checked the time on my phone: 3:21.

"Where are they?" my husband asked distraughtly as he turned to make another lap.

I calmly replied, "I don't know. I tried to call again, but I don't think they hung up the phone, so my call won't go through."

"I can't wait much longer. I'm going to drive myself."

"You can't," I replied evenly.

"You won't wake up the boys!" he moved toward me, equally desperate to protect them from his current state. "And I have to go," he stated quietly.

I kept looking in the distance, waiting for help, becoming convinced it wasn't coming, and fearing I would be left on the porch, alone, to wonder about the safety of my husband—and others on the road, given his current state—but unable to leave my children at home alone. I stood and watched as he took the keys, got into the car, started it, and backed into the turnaround in our driveway. I inhaled deeply, surprised at the composure I maintained. I sent a prayer heavenward containing no words, a plea. The car drove up the driveway, stopping seventy-five feet later at the walkway to the porch. Jay got out. "I can't do this." I exhaled slowly. *Thank you*.

"I don't know where they are," I mumbled, arms raised in frustration and then hanging in defeat. "Do you think they went back to bed? Who can we call?" It had been almost thirty-five minutes since Jay had woken me. I felt abandoned.

"Can you call Scott?" I suggested, knowing Jay's younger brother slept within reach of his cell phone and was only a couple of miles away. I was aware that Jay did not really want anyone in his family to know what was going on, but was equally aware of the desperation that had started to creep into my own voice. I could not continue to watch my husband struggle for much longer, nor stand calmly, but helplessly, on the porch in the dark.

He took out his phone and called his brother. A short conversation later, he hung up, nodded that help was on the way, and we both got into the car to wait. Jay continued to shake and struggle. I sent a small reassuring smile his way, as I knew that in mere minutes I would be able to finally *do* something to help.

The next set of headlights slowed at our driveway, and a truck, my helpline, pulled in. Scott got out, and Jay briefly explained what was going on. I waved as we pulled out of the driveway. I was feeling less helpless now, but still abandoned, despite the fact that our kids were now cared for.

The ten-mile drive to the hospital was a long one for Jay, as his agitation grew the further we went. "Do you see why I couldn't drive myself?" He smiled at me, hands still shaking, body shifting, breathing labored. I smiled back at him, noting how similar this night drive was to the last two hospital runs to deliver our children—our roles now reversed.

"We're almost there." I patted his shoulder in much the same way he had done for me as I struggled to get comfortable, slightly shaking, breathing heavily while in labor.

We pulled into the parking lot, and I grabbed my purse while Jay escaped the confines of the car. His pacing resumed as I went to the desk to fill in the required paperwork.

As I got out our insurance cards and started to fill in the blanks, the receptionist kept glancing at Jay. He paced back and forth, breathing slowly and heavily, hands shaking at his sides. I noticed he was leaving a dirt trail wherever he walked, as he had brought part of our dirt driveway with him. "I have anxiety, too," she whispered, confiding in me. "He's making me anxious, and I can't take my medicine at work." I smiled with what I intended to be a look of empathy for her, as I hoped, for the sake of both of them, the paperwork portion of the proceedings would move along quickly.

Finally finished, we met a nurse at the door. She seemed to be both caring and no-nonsense. "Come with me," she said. She held open the door and pointed to the triage room. We entered a narrow room, only slightly larger than closet-sized, containing three chairs and a computer sitting on the counter. I couldn't imagine Jay sitting in this room at all, let alone for any large amount of time. He sat, shaking, as I answered questions.

"Is he on any medication?"

I pulled out the two prescription bottles we brought containing his new medication and explained how much he had taken in the past 24 hours. Jay apologized and got up to pace, leaving just the nurse and I to finish.

"Does he smoke?"

"No."

"Does he drink alcohol?"

"No."

"Does he drink caffeine?"

"No, he gave up all caffeinated pop and such over a month ago."

"Does he take any recreational drugs?" She raised her eyebrows and looked at my husband, the figure of drug withdrawal, who had begun pacing in the hallway in front of the door, leaving more dirt in his wake.

"No. Really," I responded to both her verbal question and the nonverbal eyebrow raise.

"I really don't," my husband responded from the hallway, evidently still paying attention.

"Any surgeries?"

"No, just some serious anxiety tonight," I responded. "Other than that, he really is quite healthy."

"Just my head," we heard as Jay walked past the door again, shaking and panting, but still hanging onto a bit of his sense of humor.

"Well, let's see what we can do for you. Please head over to this bed, and I'll be right with you," she said to the moving figure in the hall. "And if you need to keep pacing, just don't go very far." She smiled, looking at the dirt trail he was leaving everywhere he went. "Although it looks like we'll be able to find you."

I looked at the clock, 4:13. I grabbed my phone and called into our sub system. I knew that we had been having trouble getting subs lately. I was also aware that my principal and two of our teachers were going to be gone today, making it even more unlikely that I was going to get any coverage. That left only our guidance counselor, my running partner, to man the helm of our building and my classroom all day. She could do it, but it would be an awful day for her. I should go in. I realized there was a part of me that was secretly hoping no one would pick up the job.

My stomach tightened. The emotions of the night, which I had held at bay so far, were threatening to overwhelm me as I realized help was on its way, and I would be able to let my guard down. In doing so, I would then be faced with the fact that my parents hadn't come to my rescue. I was left with this new, unwelcome feeling—abandonment. I was still helpless to do anything to assist my husband, but I suspected whatever they had in mind to do in the ER was going to mellow him quickly and completely for a while. The thought of staying home and thinking about either of those emotions, let alone both at the same time, made my anxiety level soar. I did not, however, want to leave Jay, either. Still torn, only now tinged with guilt, I struggled silently.

The nurse had been consulting with the doctor on call that night as Jay continued to pace, shaking. She entered our curtained bay. "Hi. I'm Dr. Matthews," and proceeded to ask the required questions. "I'll send the nurse in with a shot, and he should settle down, perhaps fall asleep quickly. Please make sure he follows up with his doctor as soon as possible." As she drew the curtain and went to find Jay, following his dirt trail down the hall. I saw her talk to him briefly, then send him to the bed where I was sitting.

Jay walked in; the nurse followed with purpose and a needle. "Alright, show me your cheeks."

Jay laughed, "No one has said that to me in a long time," as he turned and complied. The relief he had been waiting for all night was quickly administered to his bare bottom.

"You can walk around for a bit more, but when you start to feel tired, you have to come back and sit on the bed. It will work pretty quickly." She put a hand on his arm and smiled. Then, more gruffly, "No driving and no work until after lunch today. Can you do that?" Her face grew serious, getting her point across.

"I'm fine today. My boss knows what's been going on. I can stay home, and she can drive." He pointed in my direction. "I do think I need to keep walking, though. And I will clean up my mess. I'm sorry."

"You'd better clean it up!" she chided, smiling. "Well, we weren't going to lose you, now were we? And the custodian will be here within the hour, so don't worry about it," she gave him another pat on the arm as she went to fill out her chart.

Jay paced. I checked the sub system. No one had picked up my job. I didn't want to ask him about maybe going to work.

I desperately wanted to go.

The medicine kicked in quickly as promised, and Jay came in to sit on the bed by me. The shaking finally over, I asked, "How are you doing?"

"Better. The doctor wanted to make sure I wasn't coming off an acid trip, I think," he smiled. "I did look a bit like a drug addict tonight, and I made quite a mess on the floor." He looked down at his dirt trail. "I'm really sorry about this," he quietly added as he slowly looked up at me.

I smiled and chuckled. "Nothing to be sorry for, Sweetie. Except for the mess you made." I squeezed his hand. "We'll be ok."

We sat in silence for a bit. "Sorry about the hold up in getting someone to the house. I'm glad Scott was able to come over."

"What happened with your parents?"

"I don't know... I'm sorry about that. I'll figure out what happened." I took a slow, deep breath, checking my emotions, fearing they would all tumble out at once, and I wouldn't be able to pack them back in. "I'm sorry you had to wait so long... I'm angry... How are you really?"

He smiled, "That's some pretty powerful stuff they gave me. I'm getting pretty mellow. And tired."

"Do you think you'll do lots of sleeping today?" I looked for a sign, trying to gauge the probability that my next request was a fair one to ask. I proceeded cautiously. "I don't have a sub, and I don't think I'm going to get one. Paul and both Jeremys are going to be gone today. How do you feel about me going into work if I can get the kids where they need to be? I think I can get someone to cover my class to start the day. Tracy can't cover the office and my room, too." I waited for his reaction, hoping I wouldn't have to sit at home all day, yet feeling guilty about even asking. "I can wait until six to see if someone will still pick it up, but I really don't think it's going to happen."

"That's fine. I imagine I'll just sleep for most of the morning.

What are we going to do with the boys, though? I'm supposed to drive the preschoolers today. I'm not going to be in any shape to drive. What about getting Tristan off the bus in the afternoon?" The logistics of our current state in life were growing more complicated the more we thought about it. I began brainstorming solutions that required nothing of my husband and still got me to work within an hour of the starting bell. I looked at the clock. It was just after 5:00 a.m. This was going to be a long day.

The medication relaxed Jay's taxed system, while I began to plan. I would have to drive to my parents' house to see if they were able to watch the kids during the day—as I still couldn't call. I wasn't looking forward to that conversation. I was still angry, a safer emotion than my feelings of helplessness and abandonment. I could call my friend, the high school math teacher, to cover my class, as he had a first hour prep, and I had asked for his assistance yesterday on the project we were working on. He knew what to do and would be willing to help me. I could drop off all of the kids at preschool and still get to school by nine. I would have to see if Mom could pick them up at lunch, but I didn't think it would be an issue. Tristan could get off the bus at our house for an hour before I got home. Jay would be home if he really needed something, but he would be more than willing to play Wii for an hour without the distraction of his brothers. I would need to write a note for the bus driver. I wasn't sure if all of the school bags were packed, and the clothes weren't laid out yet, but I still had time to do that if necessary. Sleep wasn't going to be in the cards for me in the near future. I could get everything in order, though. I could go to work, an idea I was now clinging to as though my emotional well-being depended upon it. Perhaps it did.

We got the ok to leave. While walking out of the hospital, I explained my plan for the day, taking care of the details before going into work, checking both to make sure it was ok and to verify that I hadn't forgotten anything. We rode home in silence, my mind full of the events and emotions of our early morning, and his in a drug-induced fog.

At 5:30 a.m., we pulled into the driveway, thanked Scott for watching the boys, and headed in. The boys would remain unaware of the events of the night. Jay headed upstairs to rest. I briefly considered lying down, but thought better of it, realizing a nap at this point would only make me more tired. I decided not to make sub plans unless someone actually picked up the job. If it got to be six, I would begin to execute the plan for the day, making the trek to my parents' house to figure out what happened and to ask them for help. In the meantime, I sat in a chair reading, filling my mind with words from the page and keeping my emotions at bay.

The clock moved to the appointed hour. I checked the sub system one last time, found myself thankful that my job was still open, but wondering exactly how the conversation with my parents was going to go. I stopped upstairs to check on Jay. He was resting quietly, the shaking finally over. "No one picked up my job. Are you sure it's ok for me to go in?" I checked one more time, trying to keep the desire to go to work from my voice.

"As long as your mom can help, it should be just fine. I'm just going to be up here most of the day anyway," he responded, drowsily. "Make sure Tristan knows to get off the bus here."

"Are you sure?" I asked again, needing reassurance.

He smiled, sensing my plea to leave, "You should go."

I kissed him. "Ok," I took a deep breath. "I'm going to drive to Mom and Dad's then, as I still can't call." I closed the door quietly behind me and prepared to talk to my parents.

I pulled into the driveway, unsure of both my expectations and my response for the conversation I wished didn't need to happen. I turned off the car and took a deep breath. I wanted to stay angry, as abandoned was still too new and raw for me to face. I got out and walked up the sidewalk.

I knocked twice, sharply, and walked in. My parents were both standing in the dining room—the same odd look on both faces. They were waiting for me, equally unsure about what was going to unfold. We all stood silently.

"Did you call last night around 3?" Mom asked tentatively.

"I did," I answered, checking my emotions. "Jay had an anxiety attack, and I needed to take him to the hospital. We needed someone to watch the kids." My voice sounded monotone and detached. I had a long list of things to do this morning, however, and emotional meltdowns had not made the cut. Dad tisked and hung his head, the realization that all was not well between us now confirmed.

"We didn't know if you'd called by mistake," Mom quietly stated, with remorse on her face.

I scoffed. Anger made a brief appearance but was quickly brushed aside, as I was going to request their help again. "In the future, I probably won't be calling at 3:00 in the morning unless I really need you," I stated, sarcasm masking my vulnerable emotions. "If you are ever unsure, will you please call back?" My anger bubbled again to the surface.

"Yes..." Mom began.

I interrupted, as there was business to attend to. "Scott came over. We are home. Jay is resting. I can't get a sub. I need to go to work. Will you help with the kids today?" I factually cataloged the night's events and made my new request.

"Yes," Mom replied, mimicking my businesslike tone, "I can," she answered. We dealt with the details of the day in our efficient, German way—the unspoken emotions and vulnerabilities left to the side until the business was finished.

When the day, and all of its easy-to-answer questions, had been dealt with, Dad asked, "So, what's happening with Jay?" His concern and confusion were obvious.

I realized we hadn't told them of Jay's anxiety, his new medication, or our recent struggles—wanting to handle it ourselves out of pride or fear of judgment, perhaps both. They had no idea what had been going on at our house a mere two miles away. While understanding their uncertainty over my phone call came later, it eluded me in the moment.

"It was bad. I needed you," was all I could muster, my eyes glancing up at them—angry, accusing, hurt.

The whispered reply from my mother, "I'm sorry," two sets of eyes watching me, searching for the forgiveness I wasn't ready to give.

I took a deep breath. "I'm glad you are available now."

❄   ❄   ❄

And as I pulled into the driveway of my school, singing at the top of my lungs, coping, I realized that I needed my students way more than they needed me today. I needed them to ask me questions that I could answer, needed them to be squirrely so I could redirect them, and needed them to bring some regularity to my morning. Mostly, I needed them to fill the hours of my day so I couldn't dwell, stuck on a loop of worry and anger that rendered me helpless and useless.

The cryptic message given to me as a child by my grandmother and the other women in my family finally became wisdom to learn from and lean on. I did not dwell on the events of the previous night. And only in doing so was I able to positively cope.

HALF-MARATHON:
13.1 MILES

The sweat from my forehead ran down my face and intermingled with the tears from my eyes. I wiped my face with my shirt sleeve and pressed on. To an unsuspecting onlooker, I imagine I looked just like another local runner pushing the pace. I was beginning to realize, however, that this run, like so many others this summer, had become a race against some stiff competition. Each mile marker met me with thoughts and buried emotions that I had time to spend with, whether I wanted to or not.

MILE 1: ANGER

It was the Summer of Our Discontent. Running had always been a coping mechanism for me. This summer, it had become my sole healthy outlet. Drinking also worked well, but seemed much less acceptable, as I was usually drinking alone, and it made my already sharp, biting comments even sharper—not helpful. Running, on the other hand, frequently made me too tired to continue fighting once I returned home. While it didn't seem to solve any of our problems, it didn't add fuel to the fire. There was also the added benefit of fitness, which was sorely needed after the birth of our two sons, while drinking just added to the dissatisfaction of my "mommy" shape.

We argued—frequently. Sometimes we fought loudly—anger spewing from our mouths in rushes of unmet needs and disappointments. Sometimes we fought in hushed, biting phrases—anger showing itself in whispered words meant to hurt. Sometimes we fought by saying nothing at all—anger in the silence: things unsaid, situations imagined, all unspoken. Regardless of form, Anger lived at our house that summer. To begin with, Anger showed up visiting only now and again. Staying a bit longer each time, quietly and unnoticed, as the hours turned into days. I think we both believed things would work out. Until one day, she never left, remaining an unwelcome guest.

I ran. And ran. And ran some more. Anger and Frustration were on my heels, threatening to overtake me, Fear drafting behind them. I had escaped from the chaos that was becoming my house—the negative emotions always threatening. Running, I was in control of the rhythm of each step. Pushing. I was holding them off one step at a time. I knew I could out here. Anger, Frustration, and Fear were all threatening to overtake me in my day-to-day routine, but on the road, they were no match for me. The harder I ran, the less hold they had over me. I would conquer them each, one mile at a time, freeing myself from their grasp.

Anger always seemed to come up front first. We would start together fast and furious. On the road, I was currently holding my own in the race, her energy quickly spent in the early miles. I was content to run as long as it took to move past her, setting a quick but sustainable pace. Acknowledging the emotion for what she was, Anger seemed to be the frontrunner of the other emotions—flashy and safe—quick to show herself early on, hiding the stronger emotions behind her. There was nothing positive or productive about Anger, though. She just muddied the waters. Anger was swift, but quickly faded, a sprinter in this distance race. I found my rhythm, arms pumping and knees lifting. As miles 1 and 2 passed, Anger went to the wayside, my focus changing to the next competitor.

MILE 3: FRUSTRATION

I was unhappy. There were always too many things to do and not enough time to get them all done. Before our children were born, I had energy for teaching and coaching. There was time to visit with friends, read books, and do the laundry. The birth of our second child had changed all of that. I now found myself perpetually behind. Now my friendships lapsed and the pile of unread books lay dusty, along with everything else in the house. It seemed as though just keeping everyone fed and clothed took an undue amount of time and effort, leaving precious little of either left at the end of the day.

I knew this was typical of parents with small children. I had looked forward to it, though, welcoming the challenge. Our eldest child, just over the age of three, and our infant, quickly approaching his first birthday, were adorable, entertaining, and the loves of my life. They were also demanding. Their boundless energy and curious natures meant there were messes to be cleaned and dangers to watch out for. Perpetually hungry, the kitchen never closed and, as a result, was never clean. Their fickle personalities, creating emotional highs and lows within mere moments of each other, left me on edge. Mostly, they were just plain needy—in need of help with virtually all tasks, and a substantial amount of patience for those things that they wanted to complete independently.

All of this would have been easier to bear if Jay's response to our life with two small children had, in any way, matched my expectations. He had become increasingly overwhelmed, unable to deal with the noise, mess, and neediness of us all when he got home at night. Bolting upstairs after hugging and kissing us all, I was left to continue to care for the children I had been in charge of all day. There wasn't much discussion as to how long he would be up there, or why he needed to go at all. It just happened.

Believing initially we were in this parenting gig together, I quickly grew resentful of his time away, both while at work and during his escape upstairs. He had already been away from us for hours and hours! I needed an opportunity to get the housework done with both hands, instead of with a baby in one arm. I was the one who needed to get away, enjoy some personal space. I needed a break from the day. I needed to get out of the house, too. God, I wanted to get out of the house.

I continued to stew inside while smiling at my children outside. The pot lid slammed a little too hard, though, and the cupboard door swung a little too quickly, betraying the calmness I wanted to portray. My mind, despite my attempts to distract it, would begin to wonder what was happening to us. How had we gotten here? Where were we headed? Could we get back to where we'd been? Why wasn't

I enough? What in the hell was going on?

As dinner preparation continued, I arrived at some conclusions. He needed to change. I was working so hard, trying so hard. I couldn't continue dealing with his absence, both physical and emotional. It wasn't fair to me, or our children, that he was gone so much of the time. I was tired, too. He would just have to suck it up.

Dinner was almost done. I decided whatever was going on upstairs had been happening for long enough. Stomping as I climbed, I opened the bedroom door, barely noting his closed eyes and slightly labored breathing. "You going to stay up here all night?" I questioned, daring him to enter the fight I was picking. "Dinner is done. How was your day? Mine was busy," I chattered, not really wanting to listen to his answers. "I'm going on a run after dinner. I think I'm going to go long tonight." Having informed him of both dinner and my plan for escape, I walked out, not waiting for a response, and got the boys ready to eat. We did not wait for him to show up.

Frustration came quickly on Anger's heels. In miles 3 and 4, the solutions to my problems continued to evade me, as I was not looking for them. We ran in step together for a while, Frustration and I, both cocky and confident. I had hit my stride, smooth and in control. The problem wasn't mine. My commentary was justified. I knew that my sharp tongue and accusing tone of voice made me feel better, momentarily, if for no other reason than I was right.

Frustration was easy to run with. Though admittedly more persistent than Anger, I was now fully warmed up and felt in charge. The race continued as we ran side by side. I was setting the pace, my rhythmic steps self-assured and focused. Frustration smiled and kept up, showing neither any sign of weakness nor any sign she would push the pace. We ran together, happy with each other's company, secure in our current position. My mind began to wander.

As Mile 5 approached, though, I felt the need to refocus. While I was enjoying my time running with Frustration, I realized that we had settled into a pace too slow and too comfortable. Perhaps it was the fact that the solutions were right in front of me, and I didn't really like them, which was the issue. I could hold my tongue. React more lovingly. Or just be more loving to start. I could ask questions instead of just making statements, most of which were judgmental, accusing, and selfish. Although all of those solutions would help my marriage, they sounded like work.

If I were going to move up in this race, however, that is what I was going to need to do. Frustration, while easy and comfortable to run with, was also not going to help me get to where I wanted to go. I acknowledged my competitor for who she was—a comforter allowing me to become complacent and preventing me from seeing the challenge before me as mine. If I allowed her to, she would not only continue to hold me back, but also prevent me from racing where I belonged. I picked up the pace, leaving her behind.

No sooner did I leave Frustration's side, however, than another competitor, even tougher and harder to handle, took her place. I again made the effort to move ahead, the strain of the race starting to show. I began to question myself and my ability to persevere.

MILE 5: FEAR

There was something wrong. Of course, I had known for some time that our relationship could be better. We were fighting, or avoiding each other so we would not fight, on a regular basis. The problem wasn't our marriage, though.

I had been so self-consumed that I had missed all of the signs: the eyes darting, trying to find a place to go; the muscles tense, ready to flee, never relaxing; the slow, heavy breathing when I interrupted his time away; the pleading in his voice that he would need just a few more minutes. Jay was struggling with something, and I, selfishly, had left him to fight alone.

I was both afraid of what I was refusing to see with him and afraid that whatever "it" was would be too big to handle on top of our already full life. I might tumble, falling into a jumbled heap like laundry from the opened dryer door. Who would take care of everything if we *both* fell apart? I feared I would be weak and cowardly if I felt compelled to leave when the worst of the "for better or worse" was bigger than me. What if I couldn't be enough for everyone?

And why was all of this about me? I had been taught that love was other-centered my whole life. I had spent most of my summer days feeling sorry for myself, for my situation—*entire* days. I was not centering on anyone else, just myself. Did I even know how to love?

Fear seemed to be gaining steam. I couldn't seem to escape the fact that I was afraid my marriage was crumbling. A reality made worse by the fact that both of my grandparents had celebrated their 50th wedding anniversaries, and my parents were past 30 years of wedded bliss and going strong. The fact that my examples were so good made my potential failure, in my eyes, that much worse.

Fear was a force to be reckoned with. I was just trying to keep up, fighting to stay on her shoulder, making sure the gap between us didn't get too big. I didn't want to get left behind.

I was afraid that I wouldn't be able to make it on my own.

Hell, I couldn't even make it the whole day without wanting to run away from my house and my kids. Single-parenthood and I would not get along well. I was fooling no one. My children would suffer. And, too proud to ask for help, I would not fare much better. My pace slowed in mile 6, as the tears gathered in the corners of my eyes but would not fall. I could not dwell here, currently being pulled along, or I would fail.

I had to outrun Fear or I would be in her shadow, forever, left alone and less than I should be.

Pushing the pace, then, was my only choice out here as I approached mile 7. I was not confident that I could continue to move forward faster than my current pace. I was certain, however, that it was my only positive option. I must choose to deal with things differently. If I could not get past my apprehension, then I could not face the real issue in our marriage. Our marriage could not withstand the burden of Fear. I quickened my stride, pumped my arms, and moved on—leaving Fear in my shadow.

MILE 7: TRUTH

He asked me to take a drive. We were thinking about buying a truck, and he had found one an hour away that he wanted to look at. His mom would watch the kids. We could get some lunch.

I yearned to go on a date with him. We could pretend that life was back to normal for a bit—a date would fix things. All would be right with the world again. He could make me laugh. He could make me happy.

The drive was uneventful but pleasant. We were enjoying small talk and joking around, deciding by silent consent to avoid the usual heavy topics.

Once we arrived at the dealership, we decided the truck was decent, but I didn't really care whether we purchased it or not. I was excited not to be fighting. We were just appreciating each other's company. It seemed that when the life stuff was put on the back burner, we still really liked each other.

We left the dealership and decided we still had time for lunch. We were seated quickly; the waitress took our order and brought out our drinks. We settled into the silence, a sense of normalcy set in. "This is nice," I said, smiling.

Our eyes met across the table. "Yeah, we needed this," he responded, a half-smile appearing, as only the left corner of his mouth moved.

As we sat in comfortable silence, the atmosphere slowly changed, settling over us like a dense fog.

Sensing the heavy returning, I raised my eyebrow in question. He looked away. We sat silently—neither of us wanting to acknowledge the sense of foreboding that had drifted in unannounced. Our waitress arrived with our food. Our public faces appeared, me shoving my concern away and he lifting the other side of his mouth, we both smiled and thanked her. She left. We both gazed at our plates and began eating.

I had lost my appetite, pushing around my nachos, waiting for him to get ready to say whatever he was getting ready to say. He, meanwhile, seemed to be very interested in his wet burrito. It seemed as if he were deciding if he should regain the courage he had mustered to deliver his message or delay its delivery entirely.

"What?" I asked, deciding that whatever he had to say, I was close-enough-to-ready to hear.

"What do you mean 'what'?" he glanced up.

"I don't know. You tell me. You were going to say something. Say it," I demanded, even though I didn't really want to hear "it." I was tired, however, of feeling powerless. I believed that if I could take control of the situation, then perhaps I could stop feeling so afraid. I could pretend for a bit longer that our marriage wasn't ending, or if it was that I could handle it.

Our eyes met. I could see in the reflection that he could see past my fake confidence to the fear hiding behind it. I could also see that whatever message my man-of-few-words was about to deliver had been both thoughtfully considered and well planned out.

It was going to hurt.

I felt nauseous.

"I need to do some things without you," he started slowly. "Maybe you could do some things on your own. You can go out with your friends. Spend time away from me. Maybe you could go out with Mel or something?" he offered.

I sat willing my tears to stay in my head. I glanced up at him, questioning, and quickly looked away.

We sat in silence.

He tried again. "I mean, you don't go out with your friends much anymore. It seems like you'd like to have more fun. Maybe we both could..." he trailed off.

"Why can't we have fun together?" I murmured. "Why can't you make any effort with my friends? We could do things *together*," my volume started to increase as my fear that he wanted out surfaced. "We're all married now. We could go out as couples. We could *all* have fun. Why do you have to have fun without me?" I began to cry. I looked out the window behind him.

He sighed. "That's not it." I could tell he had predicted my reaction, the reason he debated bringing it up, but he felt compelled to get me to understand the real issue. He needed it. Our marriage needed it.

"What is it, then?" I started to hiss, the safety of anger once again quickly coming to my rescue. "You can't stand to be by me or the kids lately. Sneaking upstairs when you get home. Leaving whenever you can to do whatever it is you're doing. You want *out*?" I voiced my biggest fear.

His eyes got big.

My heart pounded.

I waited.

Obviously frustrated, he blurted, "I don't want out! I do want... I NEED you to find your own way to be happy. I, obviously, am struggling to find my own. I can't be in charge of yours, too." His truth spoken, he sat resigned. I looked beyond him, and another tear escaped.

Quiet.

The couple behind me ordered the daily special, split, sour cream on the side. A plate of sizzling fajitas passed by us. I grabbed my glass and finished the last of my water, ice cubes clinking as I set it down.

We sat with our verbalized honesty, finally, on the table.

His fork pushed the last two pieces of wet burrito around the plate, moving the remaining sauce into a figure eight.

Was he right? Was I expecting him to make me happy? And if he was right, did I even know *how* to make myself happy?

His hand reached for mine, his tone softer. "I love you. I don't want to leave. I will if that's what it takes to make you happy, though. You obviously aren't now. I can't do that for you. I'm so anxious lately I can't do that for either of us, even if I wanted to. I just can't..." he faded, running out of words, his honesty enabling his vulnerability.

He sat emotionally exposed and waiting.

I was starting to comprehend.

Jay was busy fighting his own demons, largely without my support. I wasn't even sure what he meant by *anxious*. Now that it had a name, though, whatever he had been dealing with seemed to grow, pushing my seemingly petty concerns to the side. My selfishness lay exposed between us, though, naked in the harsh glare of the truth. I wanted to cover it up, ashamed. My unfair expectations, many of which were unspoken or subtly referred to while I picked a fight, seemed to be crushing him. While he was still holding his own, the burden of my insurmountable, unspoken request for happiness had become too much for him to bear. He had come to realize my expectation was a task he could not complete, even if that's what he wanted.

The waitress came with the check. I quickly ran my hand across my cheek, put on my smile, and sat with my thoughts. Jay signed the receipt, glancing at me, searching for a reaction. We left together silently and drove home.

I had been stripped of my confidence. My steps faltered. The sweat from my forehead ran down my face and intermingled with the tears from my eyes. I wiped my face with my shirt sleeve and pressed on. Tears began falling freely. I realized that the truth, the painful truth, was all that was left when my legs wanted to give out. I wiped my eyes again. He was right, I realized, as mile 8 stretched on. As much as I hated to admit it, he could not be my "everything," solely responsible for my happiness. It was my obligation alone—and I had been failing.

Fear still lingered behind me, waiting for me to slow down and join her again. I could not stay there.

I pushed on.

Truth appeared.

Believing, to start, that I only had to outrun Anger, Frustration, and Fear, this new competitor late in the race took me by surprise. Truth was confident and strong. I felt tired and weak in comparison. I realized that not only was I just over halfway done in my journey, but the toughest part of the race was yet to come. I stumbled. Mile 9 came and went. I pressed on.

MILE 10: FAITH

There was much silence. Not the dangerous, biting kind we were used to, though. The *Let me digest our conversation, and I'll get back to you when I'm ready* kind of silence.

I pondered. What was I thinking? Who was I kidding? Dealing with the truth, the painful naked truth, meant I had to deal with *myself*. I could no longer place blame elsewhere, pointing fingers and complaining. Blame was easy; ownership was not. What did it mean to be in charge of my own happiness, though? And how did I get there from here?

More importantly, what was going on with Jay, and how had I neglected it for so long? Guilt tugged constantly, though at no point did I feel like he was blaming me for missing the signs. He was trying to take care of himself—and asking me to do the same.

Much to my surprise, the truth had little to do with the state of our marriage. It was in large part my lack of responsibility for myself that was putting a wedge between the two of us.

I was in charge of my happiness.

I didn't know where it had gone, though, or how to get it back. Our marriage was in trouble, however, if I couldn't find a way to address his very real, honest request.

I was utterly unsure of what to do or where to turn. Happiness seemed so long ago, my only images contained memory's fuzzy edges. I didn't know if I could do it. Jay seemed to think I could, though. His faith in me was a start. I didn't want to hear about re-engaging with my friends during our lunch date. Perhaps in my attempts to hide my struggles from those who loved me and knew me best, though, I had isolated myself.

He had asked me to find my happiness and given a suggestion on how I might find my way back. I took a deep breath and picked up the phone.

He believed I could find my happiness. Truth was joined by Faith. As mile 10 started, I realized the race had changed. We were a pack—not competitors—but teammates. Truth remained to set the pace to our end goal. Faith nudged me on, smiling, encouraging. While I did not feel strong enough to take the lead, they seemed to think I was capable of hanging with them. With their help, perhaps I could run long enough and hard enough to eventually believe it, too. Allowing them to guide me while I held on, we all moved forward together.

MILE 11: HOPE

There were three rings. "Hello?"

I didn't waste time on the niceties. "What makes me happy?" I demanded of Yvonne, my oldest friend. "I seem to have forgotten."

"Hi." She paused thoughtfully, "So good to hear from you. It's been a couple of weeks." We both paused. I waited. "Happy?" she asked, referring to my initial question. "Well...why don't you sing again? Find a stage. Get some attention. You love music, and you're good at it. Start there."

"Hmmm... that's a good idea." I pondered her suggestion. More silence.

"So... How ya doin'?" she asked gently. She was right. We hadn't talked in some time.

"Umm... I've been better." I started slowly. "Trying to make some changes. Thought you might have some good ideas. You're the one who's known me the longest. I was hoping you might remember what makes me happy. I've been asked to work on it," I responded, opening up.

"Yeah, happy is a tough thing to hang on to," she sympathized. "Perhaps we should go out. I also seem to remember you like to dance and have fun. We haven't done that in a bit."

"I don't have anything to wear," I objected. "And I think I forgot how to dance."

She laughed gently. "So will Friday work for you? I can pick you up. Wear your cute sleeveless black shirt. We can leave after you put the boys to bed. Warn Jay you'll need a nap on Saturday."

I sighed, relieved to have a plan, "Ok. See you soon. And Yvonne," I paused.

"Yeah?"

"Thanks."

I ended the call, smiled, and went into the living room. Jay had settled on the couch, screen in hand.

"Hey, Jay?"

"Yeah?"

"Yvonne and I are going to go out on Friday after I put the kids down. Will you be around?" I asked, nonchalantly, picking up a toddler-sized underwear and shirt crumpled on the floor.

He, a bit surprised, glanced up from his phone. "I don't have any plans. I can hang out here with the kids," he responded without hesitation.

"Great... Sounds like it might be a late night. I think I'll need a nap on Saturday, too. Is that ok?" I hesitated, making my way to the clothes basket.

"Sounds great." A tiny lopsided smile threatened to appear.

I turned to leave the room. Paused, back still turned to him. "I'm going to go upstairs and find something to wear."

"Ok," he responded. "Maybe you could wear that black shirt. You look good in that one." I could sense a growing smile.

"I'll try it on. And Jay," I turned my head slightly, making eye contact with him, "Thanks." I turned and walked upstairs.

Hope, another of my true teammates, seemed to be too far ahead for me to ever catch. She, working with two others, eluded me, but perhaps only because I let them. Waving at me, but unwilling to slow their pace, they seemed eager to add members to the team. I had not yet thought of joining them.

I pushed harder.

Truth and Faith had served their time in front of our pack helping me along. As we passed the Mile 11 sign, I smiled and moved up, taking my turn at pushing the pace.

MILE 12: LOVE

My night out with Yvonne had been fun. It had not magically solved all of our issues, however. There was less fighting at our house, but all was still not well. My old habits were proving hard to break. My "happy" was harder to find than I thought it would be. I was certain I could not get to where I needed to be without some help.

"So, I've been thinking about going to counseling," I mentioned casually one night, as I washed the dishes. Jay put the last of the leftovers in the fridge, pausing slightly before he shut the door.

"I mean... I would start on my own..." Waiting, I put the last dirty pan into the water. "I think I need some help finding my happy," I continued, releasing each piece of my plan slowly, "but if we eventually think it might help, would you come, too?"

He stood up and paused again before shutting the door. He didn't turn around.

"The counselor and I, I mean... if we think your input would be helpful? Eventually... we could work together?" I was trying to ask for help without letting go of the responsibility I now knew was mine. I was scared.

"Yeah, I could probably do that. Eventually," he responded without making eye contact and started to walk away.

I stood, looking at him, not totally satisfied. While his verbal answer was the one I was looking for, it did not match his non-verbal body language.

I wanted to keep talking.

We should talk about it. A lengthy, drawn-out discussion—of many words.

I had gotten the answer I was looking for, though.

I resisted.

I dried my hands. I kept my mouth shut.

I did not want to.

He turned, glimmer in his eye, "No, commentary? He smiled. "Wow. Look at you go."

"You are a jerk!" I threw the towel at him and walked over to face him. "I say all of that hard stuff, and all I get is 'eventually'?"

His eyebrows raised in fake surprise, "Isn't that what you wanted to hear? Or were you hoping for a long, heartfelt conversation? Sounds like we might have a few of those in our future." His eyes rolled as his lips smiled.

I hugged him, sighing a breath of relief. He hugged me back.

I took a risk and moved forward. I didn't know if I could keep up this pace, but I was willing to try. Without slowing, Love turned to me and smiled. We were traveling at a pace much faster than I could manage on my own. It was in working together, though, that I realized the power of working as a team. Our synergy, while still challenging, created a euphoric atmosphere that made it possible to exceed my dreams. We turned onto Mile 12 with a new vigor, gaining confidence in our cooperation. The finish line, attainable but still a ways out, motivated our movement. While a part of the race the whole time, I had allowed Love to elude me. Freed from the comfort and safety of the other competitors, I was now traveling faster than I believed I could. Joining my true teammate, we moved forward. It was not easy. We pushed on, our leader now within reach.

MILE 13: GRATITUDE

Counseling was not easy. I found there were many ways I had been looking for others to fulfill me. Happiness, it turns out, is an inside job—the hardest kind. I persevered. I rediscovered music and continued running, though with less anger. I forgave myself for rough days and tried again. I learned to ask for help.

Slowly, and with much practice, I found ways to notice and appreciate the many wonderful things going on in our lives. Gratitude for all the little things became my daily goal. When I made an effort to look, there were sloppy kisses and squishy hugs, beautiful sunrises and delicious meals. Good things, which had been there all along, began to fill more of my day. I found that I had more than enough. I was enough. In changing my focus, I began to change my life.

"Eventually" arrived, and Jay joined us in counseling. There were many hard conversations. We had been neglecting our relationship and had fallen into some bad habits. Some of my assumptions were incorrect. Also, I wasn't very good at asking for what I needed, and my husband, while intelligent, did not have the talent of mind reading. Jay started to investigate ways to deal with his anxiety differently. We each took ownership for our individual struggles. We celebrated our improvements. As a result, we were better—together.

Gratitude smiled as we caught up. Her look seemed to say, "So glad you could join me. Where have you been?" without judgment. Our gait shared the same rhythm—quick, steady, natural. I knew we would make it. We would be ok. We continued to push hard, one step at a time. While working together, the long end stretch became easier to tolerate. The finish line appeared.

The end lesson in our marital struggle has proven to be a hard one to master. Though I wish it were not true, finding my happiness starts anew each day. Jay and I will never be "done" working on our relationship. Joy in life, I've discovered, requires the continued practice of love and gratitude. Some days are more difficult than others. It takes diligence. I find it much easier to find fault, criticize, and blame others when I am unhappy. It doesn't take any effort at all to slip back into those habits.

In making a conscious effort to focus on the good, though, I found not only my happiness but also unearthed a deep joy that lasts as long as my gratitude.

Had we started together, Love, Gratitude, and I, the whole race would have been less complicated. Before the race, I thought I needed a value judgment like easy, better, best; Comparison was necessary, even. I learn the hard way. I suspect I wouldn't have accepted their invitation or listened to their game plan before the race, even if they'd asked. Perhaps this was my best way. I got to where I needed to be, to where I wanted to be, to where I belonged. It was in working together that we became strong and achieved more than we could do alone. As we crossed the finish line together, Joy gathered me into her arms.

ALLELUIA DAY

The end was near. Friends and relatives had been called and notified. A discussion took place between the brothers and sisters. Hospice was called and had been in the house all week. A conversation took place between Grandma and her children. They informed her that she was dying, her body slowly shutting down. Her mind struggled to deal with it.

Grandma's days following this news were filled with bits of fear, mumbled words, and confusion. She spoke of her stillborn first child, the one she did not dwell on. She frequently seemed agitated, both at the memories of her past and at her thoughts of the future. Her eyes focused on a point far beyond the room in another place and time. Her children reassured her—roles reversed in the final days—that she was loved and had lived a good life. They comforted each other, too; the struggle toward acceptance was difficult for many.

In her more lucid moments, Grandma continued to cope with impending death by tying up loose ends. I had heard stories Dad told of his childhood where Grandma had to deal harshly with him. While I found many of the stories quite entertaining, I suspect in the heat of the moment they were much less so. At one point, she looked at Dad straight-faced and open-eyed, "Do you forgive me?" she asked him, both of them realizing she was asking for forgiveness of those faults accrued over their lifetime together.

Dad, who knew he had challenged his mother on several occasions growing up, smiled and responded, "Mom, do you forgive *me*?"

She smiled back. "I do."

"Then I guess I forgive you, too," he replied.

Visitors continued to arrive, a testimony to her love and life. While there were many hard moments, the days were also filled with happy tears, music, and laughter. Grandma's past was full of stories too crazy to be fiction. While I could hardly imagine my grandmother as a lookout for the neighbors during Prohibition, the smile on her face revealed the truth of the tale from long ago.

Grandchildren brought musical instruments, hoping to elicit a smile, letting Grandma know through renditions of "You are My Sunshine" how they felt about her. Sorrow mingled with happy memories of years well lived, as fear and acceptance danced on the edge of conversations.

The days moved on, some better than others.

It had been a good day. Grandma was alert and peaceful. It seemed as though acceptance and comfort had taken up permanent residence. The gleam in her eye was back.

"Are you sure I'm dying?" she questioned. She sighed happily, "I feel so good."

"Oh, Mom, it's an Alleluia day," my Aunt Joan replied, grateful for the reprieve in the deterioration and struggle Grandma had been experiencing in her final walk toward death.

Grandma looked at her daughter, smiling. Despite the wrinkled and shrunken figure sitting in the wheelchair, Grandma's spirit glowed, radiating through the beautiful stained-glass windows of her eyes. Her body, a temple of the Holy Spirit, clearly illustrated the phrase I'd heard numerous times in church. The light of love blazed, a spark kindled from a lifetime of choosing gratitude and searching for God's blessings in all things.

Grandma sat, peaceful and accepting, hopeful in her future. She placed her hand on Joan's wrist, imparting a lifetime of wisdom in one short phrase: "Every day is an Alleluia day."

Excellent Customer Service

"Do we have an extension cord?" I asked as we drove into town.

"We're going to Mom and Dad's." His response, I knew, implied there would be several to choose from.

"Are there going to be any extension cords that work?" I amended my concern. "I mean, there will be three to choose from, but what's the likelihood of any of them working?" I smiled at my own joke.

He rolled his eyes. I could see the wheels in his head turning, though, as he realized I was likely correct.

We had spent several months starting to clean and organize the garage and back building at his mom and dad's place since his father had passed away. As a math teacher who inherently liked to look for patterns, I had noticed there were almost always at least three of everything; however many of those things didn't work. Ed, my father-in-law, was fairly good at organizing, but had an affinity for keeping things in need of repair, to be fixed at a later date, while purchasing a new one in the meantime.

Today's task would be to tame the bushes and hedges that had gotten a bit out of control. I had discovered a bigger, better hedge trimmer during our last cleaning stint (bringing the hedge trimmer total to, of course, three) and was looking forward to using it. It required power to work, however, and we had not brought our own extension cord.

We arrived. I went inside to say good morning to his mother while my husband Jay unlocked the back building in search of working extension cords and the trimmers. I then set to work pulling the weeds that had come up in the rock garden and between the squares of sidewalk leading up to the side door.

"Of course," I heard Jay mutter a few minutes later. I smiled, knowing he had found at least one cord that did not work. I continued working.

About fifteen minutes later, my smile grew even larger as I realized my prediction was spot on when Jay said, "I'm going to Wieber's." Our local lumber company, located only three blocks away from his mom's house, would have the requisite cords for the day's job. "I guess you can start with this until I get back," he sighed as he tossed a 15-foot extension cord my way.

I laughed. He walked past without making eye contact, opened the trashcan to throw in two non-working extension cords, sighed, and waved at me without looking back.

When the weeding was finished, I got to work. My new power tool of the day was just as I'd imagined, cutting the overgrowth easily. Unfortunately, my increased productivity quickly ended as I finished the only bush near enough to the outlet to trim. I sat on the step to wait.

With the continued glee at my correct prediction still showing, Jay walked up the sidewalk, two brand-new extension cords in hand. While holding onto a 100-footer, he threw a 50-foot extension cord my way. "Here, let's see if we can get something done."

"Wait. There are still three extension cords," I observed, smirking. I whispered, "This is how it happens."

"Mmm-hmmm," he muttered, barely acknowledging my persistent prodding. "Why don't you go work," he pointed at the end of the walkway, "over there? Away from me."

I chuckled, plugging in the new, shiny, red cord, enjoying our playful banter and my continued wit. I glanced at my watch noting we were getting a much later start than I'd hoped. I set to work.

I marveled at the new equipment. While we had quite a bit of work ahead of us, I now had the right tools. I cut the newly grown tops effortlessly. I knew I would have to do some additional shaping this year, as I had been in a rush last year and this hedge had started to crowd the sidewalk. Despite my concern, the thicker side branches cleared with ease. I switched the cord to my other shoulder as I set to work on the other side of the hedge.

I leaned over.

The cord fell.

Onto the trimmer.

It cut through the new, shiny, red plastic coating with ease.

The trimmer stopped. It sparked and thought about becoming a fire; one large flame burned for a second. I briefly considered my limited knowledge of electrical fires. It smoked. Stopped.

"Really?" was my only verbal response, quickly followed by an audible sigh. I was initially proud at my lack of cursing. Then reality set in that I would have to tell Jay, whom I'd been picking on all morning, that I had ruined the brand-new cord.

I looked at my watch. We owned it for approximately six and a half minutes.

"How's it going?" he wandered over, already having correctly guessed the order of events in the last minute.

"So, I may have nicked the cord. Do you think you could put some electrical tape on it?" I suggested, remaining in denial.

"Did it spark?" he asked. Picking up the cord, he looked at the blackened hole and exposed wires. He looked at me, shaking his head, "Kinda looks like you had an electrical fire for a bit." He dropped the cord and walked away, "Go to Weiber's and ask for a female end. My wallet is in the truck." He continued walking back to his portion of today's project, resigned to the fact that it might never get finished.

I am certain his intent was for me to drive the truck there. I, however, had no intention of arriving at Weiber's until the time of ownership had elapsed into at least double digits. I could also sense a growing frustration from my husband, which I knew from experience, was best given the gift of time. I set out, wallet in hand, at a leisurely pace.

Three blocks and three minutes later, I walked up to the counter. The man at the counter smiled at me, "How can I help you today?"

I smiled back. This was not the first time I had stood at the Weiber Lumber counter ready to rectify my mistake. I was confident not only in my ability to accept the humble pie that was coming, but was also confident in the gentle manner in which it would be served. "I need a female end to an extension cord, please. Could you tell me where to look?"

"Sure. They are right over here," he moved away from the desk. I followed.

"What kind are you looking for?" he asked pleasantly, hoping I was sent with enough information to make the right choice.

I, having already had several life experiences in this store to draw from, turned to the shelves behind us and pointed at the extension cords. I glanced at my watch. "My husband bought this extension cord about twelve minutes ago. Could you help me find one that would fit on that cord?" I smiled, hopeful in his reaction.

He smiled back.

There was no laughter, no condescension. Not even an eye roll. Without skipping a beat, he said, "Well, I think you want this one then," as he pulled the plug out of the bin. "Will there be anything else?" More smiling—no judgment. I love this place.

If he wanted to pretend it was totally normal to sell someone a replacement part within fifteen minutes of initial purchase, then I was all for it. I smiled back, "I am hopeful that is all we will need from you for the rest of the day." We walked back to the counter together.

He rang up my purchase. I willingly paid the $4.37 required to recoup my pride. "You have a great day, now," he said as I picked up my small brown paper bag and receipt.

"Oh, I intend to," I responded. "But I hope I don't need to see you again." I smiled.

He laughed at my joke, without seeming to laugh at me. I wouldn't mind coming back today if I had to, though. A true sign of excellent customer service.

BEST HAIR DAY

I was looking through my childhood photo album. As I turned the page, I realized I'd been alive long enough that the glue holding the pictures in place was failing. I turned the page carefully, trying not to upset the order my mother intended when she put the book together. After one more turn, I found it. Well, where it was supposed to be. Instead of the picture I was looking for, there was empty space. Despite its absence, I pictured it in my mind, and it flooded me with a memory.

The picture looked idyllic, a father and his daughter working together. We were outside, both of us working in a trench, laying cement blocks that would soon be the corner of our new garage. A team. Dad was wearing his typical work jeans, T-shirt, and billed ball cap. I was facing away from the camera in a red and white striped pair of shorts and red T-shirt, my hair long and big. My legs looked athletic, as I had recently become a three-sport athlete in our small high school. I was obviously not a woman yet, but there were more than a few hints of maturity in my slender waist and arms. Anyone looking at the picture might think that we were having a happy moment, working on a family project. We were not. I remember.

It was the early '90s. The feathered height of my hair, held firmly in place by a copious amount of Aqua Net, had reached a level of perfection that was rarely attained during my freshman year of high school. We had just gotten back from church, where there were precious few peers in attendance. I was hopeful we would have plans to go out and about today, with the opportunity for additional people to notice my fabulous hair day.

"I'm going to need your help laying block in a few minutes, Cari," Dad mentioned as I walked in the house.

"What?" I questioned, certain I must have misheard him. "Can't we just wait until tomorrow? I mean, it's Sunday. The Lord's day. We aren't supposed to do work, which I'm certain includes manual labor," I argued, my hopes for my beautiful hair having additional witnesses now at risk. Not only would people not see it, but it would be *ruined* with the breeze and potential sweat-inducing task of laying big cement blocks for our current family garage project. The thought of pulling it up into a ponytail after all of my hard work this morning, unthinkable.

Ignoring my plea to live the life God intended, he responded, "Change your clothes. I'll meet you out there." He walked into his bedroom to change. The discussion was over.

I waited one more second before turning with the knowledge that his statement meant I would be laying block, despite any power of persuasion I might throw his way. I yelled, frustrated, "Ahh!" and stomped up the stairs.

When I got to my room, my vanity mirror reflected not only my perfectly teased bangs, but the impressive height I strove to achieve every school day. I looked lovingly one more time at the perfection of my bangs and poof of my sides, knowing it potentially wouldn't look like this again for a very long time. I slammed my hands on the vanity, the main shelf of which had a slight layer of dust and random hairs, adhered by a noteworthy lacquer of Aqua Net, evidence of the regular effort I put into my hair. Sighing, I stood up and begrudgingly changed my clothes. I took one last longing look at my locks and stomped downstairs.

"There sure are a lot of boys here who could be doing this job," I said to no one in particular, hoping the suggestion would find sympathetic ears.

"Dad's already out there," Mom mentioned as she walked out of the kitchen and past me. "You'll be fine."

While eye rolling to the face of an adult was not allowed in our house, there was nothing to stop me from doing so after Mom walked by. I grumbled under my breath, put on my shoes, and headed outside.

Dad had already mixed some cement and put a pile on a 2'x2' board so we could have easy access next to us. Pointing to the pallet of blocks a few feet away from the southwest corner we would be working on that afternoon he instructed, "Let's get a few of these set up along the edge, so we don't have to walk around too much. We don't want to get worn out on this beautiful Sunday afternoon." The corner of his mouth raised just a bit. Not making fun of me, so much as making it known he'd heard my complaint and acknowledged it.

"Yeah, we wouldn't want to work too hard on Sunday," I replied with a touch of sarcasm, not enough to get me into trouble, but enough to make sure he knew I still didn't approve of this stupid excuse for family time on the Lord's day.

"It won't take too long if we get started."

"We'll work just long enough for my hair to look terrible," I murmured, not sure I wanted to admit, loudly enough for him to hear, my vain reason for pouting.

Twelve blocks along the edge of the trench, and a touch of sweat along my hairline later, I stepped down into the hole, grabbed a trowel, and set to work. I sighed, "Now what?" knowing without being told that I would be using the trowel to place the wet concrete along the edge of each side of the block. Enough to make sure there were no holes, but not so much that there was a bunch of waste to fall into the trench. Once we were both satisfied the amount was sufficient and would stick, Dad would flip the block down, tamp it with his own trowel, until it was level with the chalk line. While doing so, I would scrape the sides of excess cement, making sure it went back on the board where the pile of concrete waited for its turn to become a part of the project.

"Well, why don't you get a bit of cement on the block, and we'll get 'er in place. You can double-check to see she's level with the chalk line. We'll be done in no time," he responded with the predicted directions.

"How many rows do we need to get done today?" I asked, trying to gauge the level of angst needed to get me to the end of our task.

"Oh, let's just get started and see how it goes."

Honestly, I'm not sure if Dad could have given an answer I would have liked, other than to decide he was just kidding about our afternoon project. "Fine," I responded with a tone that could only be interpreted as *definitely not fine* and a slightly pouty lip.

We put another block in place. The breeze blew my bangs back. I could feel the height leaving my hair as the wind died down. *One brick down and a thousand to go,* I thought. I sighed loudly again.

"What would you have me do?" he asked quietly. "I have workers coming in the morning. If the corners aren't done, then they won't have a place to start, and I'll have to pay them without them doing much. I'm doing what needs to be done."

Perhaps Dad didn't really want to lay block on Sunday either.

I shrugged. My throat tightened. "I don't know," I whispered. We worked quietly finishing up the last block needed for that row. We moved the chalk line to level the next row and laid the corner block, starting another.

We worked in relative silence, finding a pattern to our work. Dad lifted the block into the trench, I applied cement, and the block was put in place. Repeat. Over and over as the breeze blew slightly, and the rows were set one after the other.

We were an efficient team. Our work was good.

"We don't get to do this much anymore. You're getting pretty busy now that you're in high school." Dad smiled, enjoying our time together. Our rows were straight. I had finally stopped whining. I even had to admit, though not out loud, the breeze was quite lovely now that I'd given up on my hair. "This is nice," he sighed and grabbed another block.

"Sure," I begrudgingly admitted, a smile hinting at the corner of my mouth without actually making an appearance. I wasn't going to actually say anything, but it was possible, looking at our progress, that I hadn't hated *every* minute I had spent outside that afternoon with Dad.

Our peace was short-lived, though, as I noticed Mom out of the corner of my eye. "Mom! Why are you out here? And why do you have the camera?" I looked at her over my shoulder for emphasis and then turned away. My frustration ratcheted up to new levels instantaneously, tears filling the lower brim of my lashes. My hair was going flat. My hands were dirty. I was stuck doing a job I didn't want to do. And all Sabbath rules were being completely ignored. Now my mother wanted to document this fabulous hair day turned bad. "I think we'll want to remember this," she said.

It seemed ignoring all of my pleas was the order of the day.

"Yeah, right," I scoffed, refusing to look at her. She took the picture anyway.

❄ ❄ ❄

"Hey, Jay, I'm looking for a picture of Dad and me. We're laying block for the garage. Have you seen it?"

"Isn't it in your photo album? I haven't seen that picture in years," he popped his head into the room. "I know which one you mean, though. You aren't even looking at the camera, right? Laying the foundation. It's like the best summary of your relationship with your dad in one photograph."

"Yeah, that's the one. But what do you mean 'Best Summary'?" I asked.

"You know what I mean," he responded, leaving the doorway.

I followed into the hall, annoyed, as I sensed he was right, but I couldn't quite figure out why. "Actually, I don't know what you mean, which is why I asked. How is that picture the best summary of our relationship? I was super annoyed that day, by the way. It's not the happy picture it looks like."

"I'm even more right then," he chuckled.

"I'm sure you are," I conceded, hoping he would keep talking. "But tell me why." I got in his way, arms crossed, waiting for more.

He sighed, stopped, and, seeing my expectant face, realized I wouldn't let it go until he answered. He paused, thoughtful, and then explained. "It's the fact that you're the only ones out there working... showing his trust in you to get the job done, and symbolizing how close you two are, with you being the firstborn and the 'go-to' when stuff needed to be accomplished. He found you trustworthy. Also, though you're facing away from the camera, according to you all grumpy, I don't think either one of you were looking 'happy', but you were out there on a Sunday to get done what needed to get done. It may not have been fun, but it was necessary." He stopped and smiled. "And just because you don't look happy doesn't mean you aren't content."

He stopped, to see if I was going to disagree.

I did not. My silence spoke for itself. I remained with my arms crossed, waiting for him to go on.

He continued, "Not pausing for the picture, neither one of you had time for that. It seems like you're saying, 'Just take the picture and let us keep working.' Both of you showing love for each other by not wasting time openly arguing, which would be easy, but just gritting your teeth and doing what needed to be done. Unsaid thoughts were understood between both of you, and that was enough," he chuckled. "And then there's you in silent protest with your perfect hair exposed, showing him that, while you are out there helping, you're not happy about it and would rather be elsewhere, showing off your huge hair and ongoing womanly maturation," he smiled, eyebrow raised, daring me to disagree with his assessment.

"Hm, that's a lot of things to think about a picture you haven't seen in years," I responded, both impressed and annoyed by his astute observations of a photo he hadn't seen in a very long time. It was a wildly accurate description of the relationship he'd been witnessing for decades.

I am sad I can't find the picture. Though it seems my memory doesn't require it. And now my heart knows why it keeps coming to mind. My hair really did look good, even from the back.

FUNERALS

Most people would rather have their fingers pulled off one digit at a time than be required to attend a funeral or visit a funeral home, but not my father. He loved a good funeral and, throughout my childhood, felt the need to bring the whole family along. While I eventually met several people that had never stepped into a funeral home, we frequented the place as if it were a favorite restaurant.

Living in a small town with a large extended family gave us an advantage in knowing someone close to the deceased. Dad knew lots of people as a result of family ties, business associates, and the like. Sometimes I wondered if he didn't just make a connection with someone as an excuse to go to some future wake. For some reason in Fowler, MI, people frequently die in groups of three—no lie. I'm not sure if it's an anomaly of the area or if it happens in other locations in the world, but it's considered a fact where I come from. As a result, while many of my friends at college hadn't been to a funeral home more than three times in their entire lives, I'd had the unfortunate opportunity to attend three wakes in just over one week.

It was the joy and excitement with which my father attended wakes and funerals that had me perplexed for the majority of my childhood. There were people crying, and the dead person never really looked like the person I saw in church or walking down the street. There were several flowers, sometimes sad poems. Pictures of the person and their family from times long gone—at least one of which was usually during an awkward childhood phase, which made me want to laugh out loud in a place where it didn't seem appropriate. When I would ask why we had to go, he would reply, "It's the right thing to do. Why, there's nothing better than a good Catholic funeral. It's a celebration of life." It was this last phrase that made me think my father was totally crazy.

Despite this situation that left most people feeling ill at ease, Dad always seemed to feel right at home. He knew what to say, knew it was important to be there, and knew those the deceased had left behind would remember his presence. He would often tell a story about the person who had passed away: a favorite childhood memory of a classmate, a lesson learned from an older gentleman, or a funny story about getting in trouble during their teen years. Some stories were favorites that got everyone laughing. Some were new and unheard. It was as if Dad were giving them the gift of a memory. It was talking to those grieving about how their loved one had affected my dad's life that always surprised me and left me baffled at his upbeat attitude toward death. It was the looks of appreciation, though, from those family members that stayed with me long after we left the funeral home.

I, on the other hand, felt anything other than comfortable on these regular family outings. I felt obligated to hug people I didn't know very well and never really knew what I was expected to say. "I'm sorry" didn't seem appropriate, as there was nothing I could have done to prevent the death. I would hear other people say things like "She's in a better place now," or "He suffered for a long time and now it's over." While those things were probably meant to help or be some sort of consolation for the grieving, they seemed anything but to me. If that were my beloved family member, the thought of losing him would not be made better by any of those statements. If anything, I became annoyed and angry for those grieving individuals who had to listen to those horrible words, as giving up time with my loved one—regardless of the reason for his death—made my top three list of things I dreaded the most in life. For my entire childhood, the thought of losing my father was number one, so his zeal at attending yet another wake for someone else's mother or father, brother, friend or coworker left me in a state of confusion and wonder at his mental state every time.

My father's enthusiasm for funerals began to make a bit more sense to me as those family members close to my father passed away. Starting with Grandpa K, who had been sick for a long time—really long, it had seemed. He was in the hospital for a while after he had suffered a heart attack. I remember that Mom and I would take turns going with Dad to visit, making the trek to Lansing once a week.

Grandpa Leo and I shared a birthday, so growing up, I was always included in the family birthday festivities. He always loved his birthday, so the party was a big deal for him, and by association for me. It was this special connection with Grandpa that I believe led Dad to include me in the visits, but the time with Dad and our conversations about sickness and dying proved to be special as well.

"How do you feel about Grandpa dying?", "We're lucky to have this time with him," and "Do you like coming to the hospital with me?" were just some of the questions and comments that Dad sent my way on the half-hour car rides to and from the hospital. I'm quite certain that my replies were mostly, "I don't know," and shrugs, as these were big questions for my ten-year-old mind to ponder, let alone respond to.

I remember sitting in the car, looking out the window, shrugging my shoulders as only a middle-schooler can. These questions always led me to think about death, sometimes resulting in quiet tears running down my face. I didn't want to do that in front of my father, who loved a good funeral. I, however, did not. I found them just a sad event to dread—and suspected one was on the horizon.

When Grandpa finally came home from the hospital, the family took turns going over to Grandpa and Grandma's house, tending to his bathing, feeding, and medicine-taking. Grandma was always there, but her tough and loving 4' 10" frame had met its match, as Grandpa's sheer size was more than she could manage. It was here, as Grandpa's final days came closer, that I really saw the grieving process begin.

In his younger years, Leo was a towering dairy farmer who could fill a doorway with his very presence. Now the little things that he could no longer do—get up without help, chew the apple pieces that he used to cut up and eat in his big green La-Z-Boy chair on Sunday mornings—spoke of his failing health and brought about thoughts of death. There were sad looks in the eyes of some of my aunts, as they needed to do yet another thing for him that yesterday he could do himself. There was even a tear or two that rolled down a cheek quickly to be whisked away as the next chore needed to be done. While there were no displays of wailing grief, I would periodically catch glimpses of sadness and start to realize that even if my father wasn't sad about this turn of events, there were some in the family who had already begun to grieve the father they knew who was quickly leaving. Not everyone in my family was celebrating death.

Grandpa eventually became a shell of the man he was, who incessantly and loudly yelled, "Ma ... ma ... ma...," as he called to his wife, frequently for no known reason. I was amazed at the patience Grandma had in listening to that over and over and over, day in and day out, as it drove me crazy. As the end grew near, Grandpa moved back to the hospital, and Dad and I continued our weekly pilgrimages to visit. Our conversations continued, Dad repeating the same questions: "How do you feel about Grandpa dying?", "We're lucky to have this time with him," and "Do you like coming to the hospital with me?" I looked out the window. More shrugs and head nodding. More tears down my cheek. More words of wisdom, which didn't really make sense, from my father. A pit of dread filled my soul.

The day eventually came. It was three days after our birthday celebration; I came downstairs to get breakfast like any other summer morning. I could tell that something was amiss before my last foot left the stairs. "Grandpa passed away this morning," Mom said quietly. No tears. No Dad, who was off running errands and taking care of funeral business. My brothers seemed a bit subdued but were playing and eating breakfast as usual. I wasn't sure what to do. I wanted to cry, but no one else seemed to be that sad. I was torn between reacting the way I felt and reacting the way I thought I should.

In all honesty, I don't remember much of the funeral home.

I believe it followed much the same pattern as the rest of the visits from my childhood. There were pictures, flowers, and statues. People, lots of people, came to pay their respects. Grandpa was the oldest of 14 kids—all good Catholics, so there were lots of family members in attendance. He was also a good man, so there were lots of friends and neighbors as well. At one point in time, Tony asked my father, "Dad, how come you aren't crying? Aren't you going to miss Grandpa?"

"Sure, I'll miss him, but today we should be happy for your grandpa. He lived a great life, filled with friends and family who loved him. And now he has passed to a better place—today should be a celebration!" And celebrate we did. Grandpa had a packed house in church. We sang "Be Not Afraid" and "On Eagle's Wings." We drove the four miles out of town to the cemetery to throw dirt on the casket. Grandpa was getting "planted," Dad's affectionate label for this portion of the proceedings.

Right before they closed the casket and headed to church, we went up as a family to say our last goodbyes. I was red-eyed and teary, as were my brothers and Mom. I felt awkward. I wanted to get on with things. To be honest, I was a bit annoyed that the sense of celebration at Grandpa's death seemed to elude me. I was just undeniably sad. As we were about to turn away, I heard Dad sniffle—three times. We filed out of the funeral home to let the next family say their goodbyes, but before I turned all the way around, I thought I saw tears running down his face. At that moment, I thought Dad's sadness at his father's death, which had yet to reveal itself, would come out. The opportunity for recognizing my own grief in my father's reaction was there too briefly for me to catch it. I followed him out the door.

It was many years later, after I had recently started teaching, when my Uncle John passed away. He was actually my great-uncle, Grandpa's youngest brother, but only a bit older than Dad. John and his family lived less than a mile away from us, and his daughter, Dana, frequently babysat for us growing up. He was a big man with a big sense of humor and the look of the devil in his eye. We once traveled together out of state to go to the wedding of my cousin, along with my mom and dad, where he protected me from my father's pickings. We visited their house often, where I was treated like a second daughter.

At the church, I sat alone, something I'd never done at a funeral, as I had always been surrounded by my family. It was a different vantage point as I felt more like an observer than a participant, despite the fact that I was deeply emotionally tied to the man whose life we would be celebrating.

Dad had been asked to read at the funeral Mass. It went on as it always did, the tradition and familiarity surrounding me like a warm blanket. I watched Dana, his only daughter, react in much the same way as I expected to react someday—lots of tears, trying to be brave, mostly just heartbroken at the loss of her father. I wondered if there was some really special connection that only daughters felt for their fathers. It was this daydreaming and deep thinking that was interrupted by the voice of my father. Dad had started reading the intentions, the part of the Mass when you offer prayers of thanksgiving and need, when he stopped in the middle. He paused, sniffled, took a breath, and then began speaking again—and his voice cracked. It was the same sniffle I heard before they closed Grandpa's casket.

While there were no visible tears, as I sat in the back of the side aisle, it was the change in tone of my father's voice and another sniffle when I realized that my dad was crying.

I was surprised, stopping to blink and listen carefully. My dad's reaction seemed to match my own deep sorrow at the loss of Uncle John, allowing my own tears to fall. It was watching my father react with the same sense of loss that I felt inside—seeing him weep—which helped me believe my father's reaction to death was more complex than I had recognized as a child. While I did believe in Heaven, I had yet to experience the joy my father seemed to find in the hope of eternal life for those he loved when they passed away. I had always felt as though being sad made me less of a believer, as I was selfishly wishing the deceased were still here instead of in Heaven with God where they belonged. It was seeing my father, lover of a good Catholic funeral, shed tears for his beloved uncle that brought a bit more balance in my understanding of my father. I found myself crying, partially because that's what I do at funerals, and I would really miss Uncle John, but in large part because my Dad was crying, too. My father's physical manifestation of grief at a funeral finally gave me the permission to publicly show what I had been trying so hard to keep inside. While there was a great deal to celebrate as someone passed from this life into the next, it didn't take away from the pain of losing them.

It was several years later when the biggest loss yet happened. I was heartbroken. Crushed. The woman who loved me whole-heartedly, without expectation or exception, was gone.

The funeral home script played out in much the same way it always did. There were pictures of Grandma K, her family, and her children. There were hugs given. The sense of celebration was more pronounced, however, as we also sang songs that Grandma loved. Many told stories, gifts of her presence in their lives. Cousin after cousin remembered how Grandma loved them. There was a story of cookies given, "even though my mom told her not to." One of my "out of town" cousins talked of how she felt so welcomed and very much loved by Grandma, even though she didn't have the opportunity to visit as often as some of the rest of us. This unassuming woman had changed the lives of many—one cookie and one conversation at a time. Including mine. She loved me before I loved myself. I miss her.

We went back to Grandma's house after the wake. The smell of chicken soup greeted me at the door. A typical bouquet of flowers sat on both the dining room and kitchen table, her beloved flowers. The house was full of people, adults in every chair, while kids filled the rest of the spaces, just like Grandma loved to see it. Bowls of soup and buttered bread quickly filled tables and bellies. The chatter and busyness of the house grew with the crowd, like so many other family gatherings. Evidence of her love.

All of my senses were filled with reminders of her, the exception being my heart, which seemed to have emptied. I sat behind the kitchen table, a silent observer, not eating, a glass of wine in hand—a first for me at Grandma's house.

The final moments at the funeral home arrived. Dad seemed impatient, worried his sisters would take too long with their goodbyes, and Grandma would be late to church, a point he had made clear to his siblings should not happen. The routine of the day continued to distance me from my emotions. I was free to walk through the next steps without much thought, as I'd done them frequently enough in the past to know what to do next. My family and I waited our turn in line to say our final goodbyes, in order of age by default.

While I spent much of my childhood watching others for cues as to how to act, I felt no such need this time. My grief was so encompassing that I neither wondered nor cared about the others. I cried. My brothers, parents, and I stood saying our silent final words. Dad motioned for us to move along. I turned to go. I could see the tears falling freely down my father's face. He turned, sniffled, and continued to cry as we walked out and got in the car.

We got to church on time.

We exited the car. The music played. We began to file in. As we entered the double doors to the church, our families in birth order, I paused at the door, not wanting to enter.

Grandma had many Catholic priests in her family throughout her life, including a brother, brother-in-law, and a son. As a result, there were many priests concelebrating her funeral Mass, a crowd not only in the pews but on the altar as well. The casket rolled to a stop at the base of the steps at the front of the church. She was surrounded on all sides. A loving, faith-filled woman, my grandma, ringed by love.

The opening prayers were said. The incense burned. The hope of Heaven pronounced.

While my father had made it clear he wanted to start Mass on time, my Aunt Rose also had a request, asking that each grandchild, all 42 of us, would bring up a pink rose during the Presentation of the Gifts. At the appointed time, my cousins and I all went to the back of the church, where two 5-gallon buckets sat full of the pink roses Grandma loved. My cousin and I led the two single-file lines. As we passed the casket, I turned to help arrange the vase on the step before me. The procession of life and love approached, one pink rose at a time, honoring its matriarch—a symbol of beauty that clearly matched her life.

I marveled at her life's work, to love and be loved.

Someday I will get the call. The one I'm not looking forward to, the day I have to come to terms with the fact that my father will not live forever.

I will be heartbroken. Crushed.

We will celebrate the man, who taught me how to roof and raise a family, with a good Catholic funeral.

There will be flowers and pictures. My dad, growing up, is easy to pick out of the pictures of his large family, because he's the small boy who would take almost thirty years to grow into his ears. There will be some of my brothers and me, both happy and entertaining, while others will be just plain embarrassing. There will be a number of my father and my mom—sweethearts to the end. All will show the deep and undying love of a man, his family and friends, and a life well lived.

My brothers and I will be standing in various parts of the funeral home, so no one will have to hug any of us they don't know. There will be lots of people—lots. This is an added bonus of growing up in a large family, my father once noted, because they are obligated to show up. Our family, however, will want to attend as well as a long line of friends and past employees who will have had, at some point during their working days, a conversation about how important it is to attend funerals to show your respect and celebrate—a fact I suspect many of them wondered at while working for him as much as I did while growing up. It's possible the line will go out the front door.

I will be teary-eyed, as I'm a weepy mourner, but I imagine I will also have a smile on my face as the events unfold. There will be stories told of my father and our family, some of which I will have heard a million times, while other stories will be new and untold— memories given to us as a gift. Some will make us laugh and some may make us cry, but they will all be about Dad, who loves a good story. The rituals of my childhood and our frequent treks to the funeral home will unfold, soothing and comforting in their familiarity and tradition.

Dad will get to church on time—a very important point. The place will be packed, standing room only, I hope, as those who know him well know that he would love for them to attend. We will sing "On Eagle's Wings" and "Be Not Afraid" as we did at the funerals of his parents. His grandchildren will bring up a pink rose during the Presentation of the Gifts. I will mourn the loss of my father and smile at the hope of Heaven. There will be a wonderful chicken dinner, per his request, after the festivities are finished and Dad is "planted." A bittersweet ending, as I'm not sure I'll ever love a funeral as much as my father. A day dedicated to a loving, faith-filled man. It will be a celebration of his life—a roofer, a husband, my dad.

Becoming the Roof:

LESSONS AS A MOTHER

ETERNITY

My father often quipped, "You can sleep in eternity." It was frequently given as a reason why we weren't allowed to sleep past 9:00 a.m. on Saturdays or to take naps past age five. Sleep was important, of course, but timing was everything. Dad was an "early to bed, early to rise" kind of guy, believing wholeheartedly you could get a lot done before noon any day of the week. Because of this, naps were a rare occurrence after early childhood in our house—not forbidden so much as strongly discouraged as a waste of good daylight. The phrase fit any number of circumstances when rest was wanted—but not really needed. Dad could be heard using the phrase when *he* was tired. It was a short, self-motivational speech he used to help him push through a project, encourage a second wind when the summer projects were piling up, or persevere when the day had been long but there was still work to be done to get ready for the next day.

Through the years, I found myself using my father's phrase a number of times: powering through a project or pulling an all-nighter in college, staying up late to grade papers as a new teacher, and repeatedly as an excuse for staying out late with friends. "Sleeping in eternity" had always had a positive connotation to it, a motivator of sorts and justification for having fun. Only later in life did I learn this phrase was a double-edged sword.

One night, our infant woke up at 11:30 p.m., ate, and promptly went back to sleep. What seemed like only moments later, at 12:45 a.m., our four-year-old needed to go to the bathroom. Next, our two-year-old needed a *snuggle* after being chased by a dragon in a bad dream for roughly twenty minutes at around 1:15 a.m. And our infant, who evidently thought that since the clock said "a.m." it was morning, woke up again at 1:58 a.m. He ate, had his diaper changed, sat in the swing, and continued to look at me with his chubby cherub-like face, with no sleepiness in sight.

We entered the darkest part of the night, just me and my son. The whole world seemed to be asleep except for the two of us. The clock read 3:17. I was exhausted. My father's statement, "You can sleep in eternity," tiptoed quietly into my thoughts. I smiled.

I sent a prayer, in the form of a question, heavenward. "I know that I can rest in eternity, Dear Father. I'm just wondering if I'm going to get any between now and then?"

GIGGLES

When I was growing up, dinner was the time of day when we were all together. Mom would create a homemade meal fresh from the garden or from canned goods preserved earlier in the year. We ate lots of whole grains. Everyone sat down and stayed seated. We would share the news of the day, listen to stories meant to impart a lesson, and enjoy family time. It was at the table where I was given questions to ponder, situations to discuss, and thoughts to explore. My parents made it a point to have us sit down together as often as possible. I gained a great deal from the family dinner table other than a good homemade meal.

Now that I had my own children, it seemed every week I found an article citing the disappearance of the family dinner table. It's causing our children to be fat, do drugs, have sex at a young age, and any number of other evils. Not only did I want my children to avoid those pitfalls, I wanted to impart to them the same important lessons my parents gave to me while we shared a meal.

Our family dinners, however, didn't quite seem to match the ones preserved in my memory. I still tried to create homemade meals fresh from our garden or from canned goods preserved earlier in the year. We ate lots of whole grains. We were seated at the table most nights of the week—seated, though, was in the loosest sense of the word.

We all had a chair, but the amount of time each person was actually connected to it varied dramatically. The only person who actually remained seated for the entire meal was our toddler, who was prevented from standing by the tray of his high chair seat, trapped. He would have gotten out if he could—I think he almost figured it out.

My husband, Jay, usually remained seated, unless I needed him to get something that was still in the kitchen, or paper towels to wipe up a spill, or help put on the pants of the newly potty-trained, who couldn't quite get them on alone.

My oldest son was busy. This was a fairly consistent characteristic throughout the day, but it was emphasized at dinner. He was frequently out of his seat. He wanted to pick up the spoon his toddler brother dropped, grab a toy immediately that'd been sitting in the same spot for two days, or punch his teasing father. Most frequently, it was for no real reason at all. "Tristan, sit down," could be heard with varying degrees of severity at every dinner.

Not only was he wiggly, he was smart, too. He could sense when my patience was about to run out, and would stop in mid-stride, "I was just going to give you a hug, Mom," he requested, batting his long eyelashes at me, smiling sweetly. Not one to turn down a hug, as I didn't think he'd dole them out quite as freely when he got older,

I allowed it, all the while scolding, "Now sit down and stay there."

In addition to this general need for constant motion, it seemed just the mention of dinner time cued his need to go to the bathroom, as the thought of adding more food to his busy little body evidently required him to make room first.

Quentin, our middle child, seemed to be following his brother's lead. He, too, needed potty breaks, or hugs, or wanted to join in the general roughhousing that happened at my husband's end of the table. It seemed as though we were never all seated at the same time for more than a mere minute during any meal.

Not only were dinners busy, but there had also been lots of talk about butts. It started with an anatomy lesson where my husband imparted the knowledge that the correct term for the lower backside was the buttock. My children found this not only very interesting but wanted to use their expanded vocabulary at every opportunity. Hitting and kicking in the buttocks had become a frequent occurrence. The offender would then say, getting the term close but not quite right, "I got you in the bud hocks!" as he ran away giggling.

My husband, finding their mispronunciation of the word thoroughly entertaining, strongly encouraged its use. It was an easy opportunity every time Quentin came out of the bathroom, bare-bottomed, as he still needed help getting his pants on. My husband would lightly tap his rear, as Tristan would tease, "Quentin, I can see your bud hocks!"

All of this wiggling and butt talk had been pervasive for a week. I was determined that, today, we would all sit down—at the same time, for more than one minute total. We would share our day, parents imparting life lessons, children taking it all in. There would be no talk of butts. I wasn't so unrealistic as to expect them to sit in rapt attention, but everyone would stay seated, eating, and the topic of conversation would be civil.

The last of the dinner dishes had been placed on the table, and everyone was in the dining room. "Remember, tonight we're going to stay *in our seats*," I emphasized, "and talk about our day. No getting up or running around. Tristan, go to the bathroom right now. No butt talk. We're going to have a nice dinner." I was confident my plan would work. I began to fill plates with potatoes and cut the steak into bite-sized pieces. Jay was getting everyone something to drink. Everyone's plate was full, potty trips were almost complete, and the expectation had been set. We said our prayers before meals, Tristan participating from the bathroom. This was going to be the family dinner of my memories.

My husband, who loved me despite the fact that I was a bit of a control freak, also had plans for dinner. I'm not sure if he had no great wisdom to impart that night, if my dinner plan was a bit unrealistic, or, most likely, if he just wanted to be a pain in my bud hocks. Regardless, before we were all seated, he began his verbal assault on my Perfect Family Dinner plan. As Tristan sat down to dinner, his bathroom trip finished, a quiet, yet audible, "Pffttt," came from my husband's mouth. "Tristan," he teased.

"Da-ad, that wasn't me," he smiled as Quentin, our four-year-old, giggled.

"Do it again, Dad," Quentin encouraged.

"Pfffttt," he sounded again, a bit louder this time, smiling. "Quentin, do you have to go to the bathroom, too?"

More giggles. "Dat wasn't me, Dad, dat was you!" he exclaimed, finding this dinner conversation totally engaging, as a new wave of giggles started.

"Do it again, Dad," Tristan cheered him on.

"How about we talk about our day, Dad?" I suggested, eyeing him sternly from across the table. "I thought we weren't going to have any butt talk tonight."

He looked up at me innocently, a mischievous gleam in his eye, "No one has mentioned the word 'butt' tonight, except you."

"Pppffftttt," Tristan exclaimed loudly, taking his cue from his father. This led to another round of giggles from Quentin, who was finding this dinner conversation the best one on record.

Jay let out another loud, "Ppfffttt!" while eyeing me, daring me to find fault with any of them, as all of the rules stated before dinner were being followed. The three of them were highly amused, getting louder, each taking a turn at making a fart noise and then breaking into laughter and giggles.

While Tristan found this dinner conversation funny, Quentin was beside himself at the hilarity in it all. As soon as he got quiet and it seemed as though the giggling would subside, someone would "Ppfffttt" again, and he would start all over. His giggle was infectious. Melodic. Innocent. It was a full-bodied, open-mouthed experience, every part of his little person bouncing with life. I couldn't even yell at him for not eating his dinner, as I could see fried potatoes every time my husband made another fart noise and a new wave of giggles began. He was the picture of unbridled happiness. Joy, unrestrained.

They had me. I couldn't prevent the smile from surfacing. It was quickly followed by a giggle.

My husband and I looked at each other from either end of the table, laughing—real laughs, not the fake, pity laugh that was earned from a bad knock-knock joke. They had followed the rules: everyone had remained seated, was eating, and had not mentioned the word "butt" once. My husband's eyes twinkled from across the table in the way that I found so intriguing and attractive when we started dating. I admitted defeat, as this reality was way better than the image I had hoped for before dinner started. We looked at our family, all giggling uncontrollably, and then back to each other. Life was good. And we both knew it.

I had fully intended to teach life lessons at the dinner table tonight, just as those I love the most had done for me. Little did I suspect that night's lesson was meant for me. I am entirely too serious sometimes. My children, with the help of their father, taught me that sometimes family is just being silly together, enjoying the company of each other. I need to laugh more—enjoy life, with reckless abandon—and what better way to be reminded than with the sound of a fart?

SORRY

Father Julius, a Roman Catholic priest and my great uncle, spent a lot of time through the years documenting family events on 8mm films. After breakfast one Sunday, Dad shared that my Uncle David had transferred a few of these home videos onto a DVD. In one of the videos, each of my brothers and I made a cameo appearance. Dad seemed excited about sharing, so we sat down to watch the younger versions of ourselves, which were now saved in digital format for eternity.

It was a slow start, as in the first part, Dad was working on the drywall in the garage. My children, who weren't terribly excited about watching people talk, were alternately playing with toys and interrupting the viewing. "Mom, when are you going to be there?" and before I could even respond, "How long is it going to take?"

"A while. Why don't you go play?" I responded as I fast-forwarded to the part of the video that was both interesting to me and noteworthy to Dad.

It was our house more than twenty years ago before the kitchen addition was constructed. My Grandma and Grandpa Schneider were sitting at the dining room table, while Grandma K, who hated being videotaped, was sitting at the kitchen table trying to get out of view of the camera. Mom was also in the kitchen, making a comment about Aunt Loretta's daughter's new illness while serving up ice cream cones. Two little boys surrounded her, anxiously awaiting their snack, which reminded me of my own children. It seemed neither she nor I could serve food fast enough when it was something as special and delicious as vanilla ice cream.

Mom finished scooping out the cones and was sitting down to eat hers at the dining room table while Grandma told a story about the time her neighbor's dog got into a fight with a skunk. My two younger brothers, who were probably six and four at the time, clambered to get into Mom's lap. She made room for them, one on each leg, as she moved her arm outside of their reach to continue eating her own cone. It looked strangely like me at dinner the night before, as my youngest, age one, desperately needed to be in my lap even though I had just sat down to eat. I, too, had made space on my lap and ate with my arm out of reach.

The home video continued as I turned to my mother, "I'm not going to get any personal space for a few more years, huh?" No sooner had the words left my mouth than my youngest climbed into my lap for the third time in less than five minutes.

"Nope," Mom said, smiling. While this was a revelation for me, it seemed my mother had known this would be the case for quite some time.

Tristan reappeared to see if the video was over yet, noting, "Hey, it looks exactly the same," before sitting in my lap to watch. He was right. The dining room table was in the exact same spot twenty years later, the kitchen counter containing a perpetual pile of mail. The only notable difference being Mom's brown Tupperware containers holding flour, sugar, and coffee for my entire childhood had been exchanged for a turntable for her cooking utensils.

"Hey, Quentin, look at you." My son pointed at the screen, thinking the childhood version of his uncle and my younger brother, Keith, was his own brother. It wasn't a bad guess. In the video, his cowlicks stood up in the exact place that my son's did.

I chuckled, noting the awkward, younger versions of my brothers did bear a strong family resemblance to the young boys anxiously waiting for the home video to be over so they could watch *Phineas and Ferb*. "Nope. That's Uncle Keith, Buddy, but they do look a lot alike, don't they?"

Shortly thereafter, my twelve-year-old self finally made her appearance. I had big hair that looked less than flattering. I found this both amusing and annoying, as I know I spent a great deal of time back then to make it look like that. It took lots of curling, teasing, and hairspray to get the late '80s hair volume I was flaunting on screen. It looked ridiculous.

Not only was my hair bad, but I was also sporting a big pre-adolescent attitude. It was obvious I had been avoiding the camera and was just shy of disrespectful as Fr. Julius asked me the same litany of questions. My posture and body language were screaming, *I'm WAY too cool for this!* as my words politely, yet stiffly, answered all of his questions. I was certain back then that I was going to grow up to be much different than the adults in my life. I don't know if I was thinking it at that exact moment, but my persona in the video made it known to all that I felt as though I were above their after-dinner conversation.

The video continued while my children became more restless and bored. "Mom, how much longer?" Tristan whined, and Kaedyn flopped around in my lap, facing me and deciding I needed a sloppy, open-mouthed kiss.

"Just a bit longer, Buddy. Why don't you go get your shoes on?"

We were getting to the end of the clip. My children continued to grow more restless and noisy, my lap continually filling and emptying of wiggly little boys. "Can I get a copy of that so I can watch it in peace at some point?" I asked while pointing at my oldest son, "Tristan, get your shoes on!"

It was as I finished this demand and turned back toward the television set that it happened. On the screen, my mother had moved to the middle of the room and sternly said, "Roger, get your pajamas on!"

With only a name change necessary, I was hearing myself. The diction, volume, and tone were identical to my own. It was the strangest feeling. I knew that it was my mother talking on the video, but it was as if I were hearing myself ask my oldest child, for the third time, to put on his pajamas. I had said it just like that last night. I am quite certain that I had just asked the same child, in the same way, to put on his shoes.

I looked at Mom. She smiled at me. We both knew at the same time. "Wow! Exchange Roger for Tristan, and I'm you."

Still smugly smiling, Mom shrugged half-heartedly, "Sorry."

Only, there was no contrition in her voice. The word was apologetic, but that's where it ended. Her tone had another message entirely. I heard, *"They drive you to it, don't they? I'd say I told you so, but I don't need to. You can see it for yourself. You were sure you would grow up different from me, but you aren't really. How do you feel about that? How does it taste to eat your words? See, I'm not as crazy as you thought. Maybe you didn't give me enough credit. It's hard to be a mom, huh?"*

And how did I get all of that out of my mother's one-word response? I've used that tone of voice, too.

BEDTIME

Bedtime at our house was frequently a long affair. We would start getting pajamas on, brushing teeth (with a mixed level of quality), and giving Dad hugs. There were kisses and, frequently, a wrestling move or two. We would eventually make our way upstairs to settle in, all three boys sharing a room to sleep.

The beginning of the wind-down was always the same: I would read a story (sometimes several), and sing a song. Before the final "prayers and thankfuls," our kid-friendly family devotionals meant to end the day, could be asked, there always seemed to be questions that had been banging around in their heads all day, or perhaps only mere minutes before the light was to go out, which would find their way to the surface. While it was rarely surprising to me how many questions and unexpected ponderings came to mind, it was frequently entertaining and sometimes informational. I learned how to do many things in my discussions with my kids at bedtime.

HOW TO IMPRESS PEOPLE AT PARTIES:

Three-year-old Kaedyn had been asking for the same story to be read before bed every night for approximately a month. (During which time, Mommy had been working on learning patience.) At the end of the story, the witch, as it was a Halloween book, burped. In an attempt, mostly to entertain myself, I showed the boys one of my little-known skills—burping on command.

After my initial demonstration, wide-eyed Tristan asked, "Mom, how did you do that? Or did you just have to burp right at the end of the book?"

"Nope. I can make myself burp any time I want to, Bud," I said, and then to prove my point, I burped again.

Giggling, "Do it again!" he requested and then resumed his giggle fit when another burp, bigger than the last, arrived on command.

And so it went, giggling, burping, and repeating for several minutes.

Tristan, who was more impressed with this talent than any other of my skills to date, demanded to know my secret. After one lesson and much practice, he too could burp on command. Some day at a party, he will be able to impress his friends, or perhaps some unsuspecting girl who has a sense of humor like his mother. We were all so proud.

HOW TO PREVENT SUNBURN AT ALL COSTS:

Once, as I was reading stories for bedtime, I looked up and noticed Quentin had a sunscreen stick, which he was applying to himself liberally. Upon further inspection, I found it had also been applied to his younger brother. I had no idea where they found it. Or why it was deemed a good idea to apply before bedtime. The good news: no one got a sunburn while sleeping.

How to deliver effective dialogue:

During one of our bedtime stories, Tristan stopped me mid-page, "Mom, you need to read that part over. See this?" pointing, "It's an *explanation* mark. It means you need to yell."

Close, Buddy. I smirked and read it louder.

How to suffer judgment from children:

Quentin was in his "I Love Dinosaurs" stage and wanted a song about dinosaurs before bed. One about a triceratops, to be exact. Not having one in my repertoire, I decided to wing it.

Me: Triceratops, triceratops, stomp, stomp, stomp (repeat) ...You have three horns on your head. You could knock down something dead... (I know, terrible. In hindsight, anything else would have been better.)

Q.: No, no, no, no, no. Triceratops eat plants. He's a herbivore.

T.: He's right, Mom. A Herbivore. Wouldn't kill an animal.

Sorry, boys. Not only were my rhymes terrible, but they weren't scientifically accurate. Thanks for the lesson. I vowed to try harder tomorrow.

How to alleviate fear with math:

Quentin was very concerned that an alien would come and hit him in the head with a hammer. There would obviously be blood all over. This led to a discussion about how likely things are to happen. Tristan thought there was maybe a 1% chance of said alien invasion. I was thinking a bit less. In response, Tristan then thought maybe -1000%. We talked about how there are no negative probabilities.

"Mom, do you think Dakota (his stuffed dog) would float if he was in water?" Tristan asked, getting concerned and hugging his favorite stuffed animal tight.

"I think he might float for a bit, Bud, but he would eventually sink if he was in water for too long."

My response brought him no relief. The thought of Dakota drowning quickly became his biggest fear. He slept on the top bunk—on the second floor. We did not live in a floodplain. We continued to discuss the likelihood of his dear dog drowning.

After much discussion, we decided Dakota could NOT go on Uncle Tony's boat, as the probability of him drowning would go up dramatically.

I had no idea my math training would come in so handy at bedtime.

How to choose potential places to live:

The child-wrangling was dying down when I heard Tristan's statement, "Mom, can we NOT move to Africa? I mean, if we move."

There was no plan to move. I had no idea where this was coming from. I asked, curious about his unusual bedtime line of questioning, "Why not Africa? It's a nice place. We aren't planning to move, but what's wrong with Africa?"

"Just look at this," he pointed to the top corner, indicating where said bug lived on each page of his *Bugs* book he had been reading all summer. "Africa, Africa, Africa, not Africa," the pages kept turning, "Africa—this one is just gross and look at how big it gets—Africa," he turned the book to me, where I saw a bug that was indeed gross, big, and from Africa, a place I had not spent much time thinking about moving to, and now had good reason not to.

"Wow, that's quite a few big, nasty bugs that live in Africa. I'll talk it over with Dad. If we move, which we are not planning to do, I'd bet we could keep Africa low on the list of possibilities."

How to not overthink things:

Every night, after all of the ridiculousness had been discussed, I tucked the blankets in around each boy one at a time. "What are your prayers and thankfuls today?" was the question with which we always ended the evening. I was frequently entertained and some-times touched by their thoughtful responses. Thankfuls often in-cluded wonderfully simple things like petting a kitten, ice cream, a favorite dinner, playing with Dad, and watching a show. Quentin, in particular, had a standby response, "My thankful is that I had a good day today, and my prayer is that I have a good day tomorrow. "

One night, after several days of the same response, a couple of which were days I wouldn't have labeled "good" as a whole, I asked, "Quentin, are you just saying the same thing on purpose? Are you even thinking about it?"

Surprised and taken aback, he responded, "Isn't that ok, Mom? I *did* have a good day. And I *do* pray for another one tomorrow." His eyes, both innocent and a bit confused, looked at me as though he couldn't think of anything to be more grateful for than today or more hopeful for than tomorrow.

"Nope, Bud," I responded, realizing that perhaps he was wiser than his mother, "those are very good prayers and thankfuls, indeed."

THE GAME

"Mom, do you want to play?" came the request from the living room.

"Sure, just give me a couple of minutes to finish this up," I said from the kitchen. It had been a busy day full of chores and small projects. I was looking forward to sitting down for a few minutes, even though I had no idea what game I had agreed to play.

By the time I got into the living room, the game had already started. They had gotten out the Monopoly board, but had adjusted the rules to their liking. Typical. Each child had a stack of $10 bills, and the car, hat, and wheelbarrow were in various locations on the board. There had been no crying or arguing up to this point. Atypical.

"What piece do you want, Mom?" asked Quentin, grabbing the plastic bag of metal tokens.

"Yeah, which one?" mimicked Kaedyn.

Tristan had already moved everyone's pieces back to the start.

"I'll count out your money."

"How do we play today?" I asked, knowing that I would only get a few rules up front and then have to figure out the rest as we went. Usually, the new rules were only spoken about after I had broken them, or when someone other than me would benefit from said addition.

"Everyone bids money and puts it in the middle," Tristan explained. "Then everyone rolls. Whoever gets the biggest number wins and gets all the money." It seemed simple. It also seemed like someone should have been crying earlier, as no one really liked to lose at our house. I dismissed my thought, as even the possibility of a sore loser in my future was better than more housework.

We all rolled and moved our pieces around the board. Kaedyn, rolling a 5 and a 6, was the winner. He bounced up and down, pulling the bills from the center of the board and adding them to his jumbled pile. The rest of us frowned.

Round two proceeded. I placed my bet in the middle, as did the younger two, Quentin adding $20. Tristan sat patiently waiting, making no attempt to add to the betting pile. He explained, "You don't have to bet, Mom."

"But you can still win?" I questioned, eyebrows raised at this new rule that seemed unreasonable and would inevitably lead to tears.

"Yeah. It's fair, Mom," he answered, justifying himself in response to my non-verbal reprimand.

"You go, Mom," Kaedyn directed and handed me the dice. I participated, eyebrows still raised.

We rolled again. I got 7. Tristan got 9. Quentin was the winner at 10. Kaedyn sighed a disappointed, "Oh…" when he realized his 5 made him the loser.

I smiled, secretly pleased that Tristan did not win. Quentin fist pumped the air, shouting, "Oh yeah!" and collected his big winnings.

No sooner had he finished his celebration than he started handing money out to his brothers and me.

I was confused.

"That's ok, right, Mom?" he questioned in response to the look on my face. He finished doling out the money. Everyone sat content, as each person's pile now contained roughly the same amount of money. "Then we can all keep playing."

I smiled, the newest rule surprised and delighted.

PEACE

As we entered the church and found "our" pew in the front row of the side aisle, I realized it was the feast of the Holy Family—a Catholic celebration of family—Jesus, Mary, and Joseph, the example we are meant to emulate. It is a celebration of the love and intimacy that comes with living together at the beginning of every New Year.

The picture of the three of them, however, in no way resembled the motley crew that followed me in the pew with an already untucked shirt-tail on our eldest child, a missed peanut butter streak on the toddler's face, and the perpetually-lifted cowlick that refuses to stay down on our middle child. I even noticed a split in the seam of the green frog backpack that had become our Mass survival pack. On the way in, Tristan grabbed a children's activity page to work on during the seated portion of the Mass. I began to suspect Mass this day, like many Sundays as of late, would become an aerobic activity.

We entered the pew, and the boys jostled for the perfect position. Everyone took off their winter coats and settled in. Tristan hunted for a colored pencil in the frog bag and worked on the maze where he picked the correct path from the disciples to Jesus. The two youngest boys pulled out the dinosaurs and began to attack each other with increasing intensity and volume. I moved our youngest child, Kaedyn, to the other side of me, hoping that a change in location would redirect his attention to another activity. It didn't work. The battle continued, only now it was happening in my lap. I, again, attempted to interfere with the dinosaur brawl and grabbed Quentin's arm. I was trying to grasp with the perfect amount of pressure—enough that he would know I am serious, but not so hard that he would scream out in pain and people would look our way, accusing me of being some sort of child abuser.

Meanwhile, Kaedyn, in his attempt to keep his dinosaur, inadvertently hit me in the throat with the large fin of his spinosaurus. I was choking, angry, and desperately trying to make it seem like everything was under control. While our boys weren't being "bad," Mass hadn't even started yet, and it felt as though I was wrestling with a tangle of octopi—and losing.

I sent an exasperated glance to my husband on the far side of the pew and sent one of the dinosaur duelers his way. The opening song was announced, and we all stood. The warm-up was over, and the workout began. Four songs left, I thought in our measurement of church time, the number of songs left to sing.

As the final notes faded, Kaedyn, who was sitting on my hip, discovered my earring beneath my hair and began to flick it with his finger. Knowing it was only a matter of time before gentle playing led to rough and painful pulling, I attempted to distract him with another toy from the bag. Tristan, who had finished his maze, turned the page to an activity that required him to find the differences in two closely matching pictures. He raised the page up, making his request obvious. I bent and whispered a request, "Please wait until we sit down, and then I will help you," as I noticed the toy meant to distract Kaedyn was about to become a projectile. I made a grab and caught the toy in mid-air. Not known for my hand-eye coordination, I looked over at my husband, who lifted his eyebrows, clearly impressed with my quick hands. The opening prayers concluded, and we sat down.

No sooner did I sit in the pew than Tristan thrust his paper into my face. "Will you help me now, Mom?" he loudly whispered.

"Yes, Sweetheart, will you give me a second to get settled?" I whispered back, trying to situate Kaedyn on my lap while Tristan slid right next to me, forcing me to put my arm around him. As both boys settled into their preferred positions, I noticed three square inches of space on the end of my knee and half expected Quentin to want to join everyone else in my lap. In a glance to my side, though, I noticed he realized this was a perfect opportunity to have Dad all to himself. Meanwhile, Tristan was getting to work on his picture, and his younger brother desperately wanted to help.

Kaedyn made a grab for the page as Tristan quickly pulled it back and glared at his younger brother. Kaedyn, not to be outdone, also glared back at his older brother with what we had affectionately named the "Stink Eye" and growled deep in his throat like a guard dog warning an intruder. Knowing this would escalate quickly, I made a grab for a slightly used activity page at the bottom of the frog backpack from weeks past. I handed the page to Kaedyn. I also found a yellow colored pencil, as any stray marks, which were inevitable, would be hard to detect. He seemed satisfied and began to color on his own page. As I had suspected early on, I began sweating.

I missed the entire first reading and attempted to sing along with the Responsorial Psalm. I vowed to catch at least part of the second reading as Kaedyn stood in my lap and proceeded to give me a big, open-mouthed kiss. Not one to turn down affection, sloppy though it may be, I hugged him, set him back in my lap, and pulled out another book. I turned my attention to the pulpit as Tristan requested I read the directions to his final activity page. No sooner did I finish than Kaedyn put his book in my face to point out the sheep in the field and the car driving down the road on one of the pages. I missed the second reading as well.

We stood for the Gospel reading. Jesus and his parents traveled to Jerusalem together. On the way home, Mary and Joseph realized that Jesus was not with them. The thought of losing a boy, even for a brief moment, didn't seem so bad to me. I reprimanded myself and refocused as we learned the worried parents went back and found Jesus in the temple teaching. I felt strangely comforted that even Mary and Joseph didn't always have it totally together. I also found myself slightly annoyed by the focus on the Holy Family, though, as the example set before us had gone from lofty to downright impossible in less than an hour.

The homily began. The crowd control continued. My goal as of late had been to gain one statement from Father's homily—only one. As the message of the day began, a book was thrust into my face and blocked my vision. I began a tale about Thomas the Train. It was terrible. I had had this same thought each of the thirty times I had read this story. I reminded myself, for the third week in a row, that we really need to exchange our book selection in the church bag.

Father mentioned something about loving each other as I noticed the toddler pulling out the hymnal and reading with such enthusiasm I worried about ripped pages. I offered him one of the board books we hadn't read yet from the frog bag and took away the songbook still intact. I returned my focus to the pulpit in an attempt to glean some wisdom about family life.

Father was talking about listening to a song, which clearly illustrated today's gospel message, but I missed the focal point. Hoping I could figure it out without his guidance, I sat looking forward to the message of the day in the unusual form of music. No sooner did the opening line begin than our middle child whispered urgently into my ear, "I have to go to the baffroom, Mom." I sent another look to my husband at the end of the pew and mouthed, "Bathroom," in the hopes that he would take him. Our oldest child, who saw a chance to escape the pew, also decided that his bladder couldn't possibly wait until the end of Mass. Dad and the two older boys left the pew as I distracted Kaedyn, lest he discover they were bolting without him.

And so I found myself, almost alone with half of the family gone from the pew, and I finally heard part of the last line of the song—something about "lasting peace." I chuckled to myself at the very idea of lasting peace in our current state in life. We fit the definition of family, but we were miles, entire continents, away from the holy example set before us on this holiday every year. I didn't get the point of the song, unless the message was the laughable idea of peace with small children. I sighed. I even thought, quite irreverently, that perhaps Mary wouldn't seem quite so serene in all of her pictures and statues if she had had three boys instead of just one.

The rest of the family came back from the bathroom relatively quietly. The older two boys sat down without poking or prodding each other. Kaedyn turned, gave me a hug, and lay his head on my shoulder, deciding his very busy morning had worn him out. The second song of Mass began signaling the offertory.

In our parish, while the ushers collect the offering, children take their gifts up to a basket set by the altar. While it is an excellent way to teach tithing at a young age, I primarily viewed it as a great opportunity to allow my children a church appropriate activity to get their wiggles out in the middle of Mass. Both boys took their dollars up to the basket, Tristan waving at Father on the way. Father smiled and gave him a small wave back. Both boys threw their money into the basket—literally—and jumped off the steps, landing loudly. As they turned to come back, Tristan grabbed Quentin's hand, and they walked back to the pew together. Jay and I smiled, as did many in the congregation, at their display of brotherly love.

They entered the pew and gave high fives to Dad for making their "basket" as well as for making it back into the pew with no undue attention to themselves, something that was not always a given. The offertory hymn concluded, and the congregation stood. We had made it past the halfway mark. I was still sweating, but hopeful, as Kaedyn was well on his way to dreamland.

As we heard the Eucharistic prayers, Jay and I switched to man-to-man defense, as now there were only two children awake. While I thought this might improve our situation, I was sadly mistaken. Jay found a ticklish spot on Quentin, and the resulting giggle was adorable. So much so, in fact, that as soon as his laughter subsided, Jay pushed the irresistible spot again, causing another cascade of increasingly loud giggles to escape. I sent my own version of the Stink Eye toward the other end of the pew, letting the biggest boy know that I didn't need to attempt to keep him in line as well. He smiled and lifted his eyebrow, daring me to do something about it. I sent a prayer toward the heavens, asking for patience and stronger lower back muscles. I shifted my sleeping babe to the center of my body as Tristan moved to the other side of me in an attempt to get in on the action with his father and younger brother.

A small miracle then occurred as both boys sat quietly on either side of their father for the remaining prayers before Communion. As song three began, we filed out of our pew. In an act of chivalry, all of my boys, big and small, allowed me to cut in front of them. We left the pew quietly and were able to return without any excessive activity. I sang quietly along with the hymn, snuggling my babe, looking at a book with Quentin, as the rest of the congregation filed by.

I sat quietly after Communion with my still sleeping toddler quietly snoring in my arms. He made a drool mark on my new Christmas shirt with a crescent of snot adorning the edge. Quentin snuggled next to me quietly as we finished the last pages of his story. Tristan, not yet too old to cuddle, sat relaxing in his dad's lap. Jay and I looked across the pew at each other and smiled. We were all content, quiet. Despite our typically taxing Mass experience, or perhaps because of it, the stillness was remarkable. Our boys, while wiggly, were wonderful and were currently still enough for me to notice. I felt at peace. I believe for a few brief moments my face may even have mirrored Mary's.

"I wuv you, Mom." Quentin, our four-year-old, looked up at me, sweetly smiling, and asked, "Is it time to go yet?"

"One more song, Buddy," I smiled in reply. Kaedyn shifted to start a new drool mark while Tristan whispered a message into the ear of his father. I paused to really look at my motley crew. They were happy, healthy, and loving. For the moment, we even passed for peaceful. We might not ever measure up to the Holy Family, but perhaps we weren't doing half bad. I'm not sure of the exact focal point of Mass, but I gleaned a meaningful message about family life. While lasting peace was still a long way off for us, there were fleeting moments of joyful contentment when I made the effort to be watchful, aware, and appreciative.

TATCHOS

He was working on his second plate of "tatchos" fresh from the microwave, melted cheese hot and slightly steaming atop his plate of corn chips. He was focused as he pulled one from the pile and gently brought it to his lips. It was hot to the touch, and he pulled it back, thinking. I sat waiting for him to ask me to blow on them to cool them down. Finding a solution on his own, he blew gently on the edge of the chip. His cherub cheeks filled, his lips puckered, and he blew gently. He looked down at the chip for the tell-tale steam showing him it was too hot. There was none. He touched the chip lightly to his lip a second time, still too hot. Fill, pucker, blow.

I watched as my not-quite-three-year-old son asserted his independence on the plate of hot nacho chips, which just a couple of days ago would have required my help to cool down. I smiled. My eyes filled with tears, held back by my lower lids and my curiosity. I watched.

He checked his chip again and, finding it cool enough, took just a nibble. He smiled, satisfied. A bigger bite was taken—another step towards independence. He was engrossed in his lunch, while I was engrossed in his every move. I wanted to stop time, to stop him from growing, to stop in this moment. I sat, wanting to clutch my little toddler and hold him, as just yesterday he was a babe in my arms.

The thought was fleeting, though, as I realized this is better – this sitting, watching, enjoying his new skill—savoring the moment. The joy came from seeing the change. Had I held him too tight yesterday, I would have missed this moment today. And so I slowed down, enjoyed it, and let it go. I filed the memory away and looked for the next one.

POKING AND PRODDING

"Mom, your skin looks old. You've got wrinkles." Kaedyn said, pointing to my belly.

"Yes, dear, that happens to mommies sometimes when they have babies. Remember me telling you how big my belly got when you were in there? It got really big," I demonstrated with my fingers barely touching the impressive girth of my belly in the late stages of pregnancy, "and these marks stayed even after you were born," I explained to the boy, weighing in at almost ten pounds initially, who was responsible not only for many of the stretch marks but also the still-separated abdominals partially responsible for my belly pooch.

"Do you have a baby growing in there now?" he exclaimed, poking at my midsection.

"Um, no."

It was the first swim of the season for me. And it was going a bit differently than I planned.

Oh, I fully intended to show off my body to my boys with my

two-piece bathing suit. At home, I was looking for ease of use in a suit, as we frequently swam more than once a day. My public bathing suit had more material—ruched, with stays, and spandex—the additional structure helped me keep things in place, things which had shifted since the delivery of my children. It also took some effort to put on and take off. More effort than I was willing to put forth on a regular basis to swim with my boys.

I was justifying my laziness this summer by convincing myself that my three boys should see what a real mom looks like in a bathing suit. There was nothing to be ashamed of, each mark earned, curves brought about by children and age were perfectly normal. Their mother, while still maintaining a fairly athletic build, would never be mistaken for a bathing suit model. However, I felt that my boys should know that their future wives might have similar evidence of bearing children. None of which they were going to find in the media or on their YouTube videos. Each child had done his part in creating the marks in my physique that were now being pointed at and critiqued. My love of wine and chocolate, and waning interest in exercise all winter long, probably didn't help matters.

In my mind, the conversation about my body slowly unfolded throughout the summer. It was an opportunity to foster necessary discussion about how their bodies would change as they grew up, to respect their body and the bodies of others. Perhaps each boy might notice something, and we could talk about the changes my body had while they were growing inside of me. We could talk about the excitement of their birth. We would possibly even be setting the groundwork for some future talks about love, marriage, and sex. While I wasn't expecting them to prostrate themselves before me in gratitude for birthing them, I was not expecting to find myself the center of an investigation. My imagination was definitely less harsh than my current reality.

"There sure are a lot of marks, Mom," he continued with his full-on examination, circling around me. He poked my belly again.

"Will you please stop?" I requested, moving his hand, already questioning the glass of wine I intended to drink later tonight.

"Are you sure there's not a baby growing in there?" he asked again, now having a hard time believing that it would stick out that far without a legitimate reason.

"I'm sure."

"Are you going to get one?" he asked as I swatted his hand away again.

"You'll have to talk to Daddy about that. I'm not sure he's up for another one. If you keep poking at my belly, you'll make me question boy number three," I teased.

From across the pool I heard, "That's not very nice, Mom," from my oldest, who was evidently listening to our conversation, even if he wasn't participating.

"You're probably right," I agreed. "And this isn't nice, either!" I shouted, grabbing a water gun and shooting the nearest boy. If you can't change the topic of conversation, diverting it with a water attack was the next best thing.

I was chronically forgetting that whenever my boys learned lessons and important things in life, I usually had to learn along with them. We were, indeed, talking about all of the things I had intended when I put on my two-piece bathing suit, though at a much more

rapid pace than intended. I had been in denial that if we were looking at the marks on my body, I would have to look, too. And if I
didn't want them to believe the media about what a woman's body
was supposed to look like, then perhaps I couldn't believe it either.
As we continued to chase around the pool, I questioned whether or
not I believed the message I was trying to send. I wanted my boys to
be comfortable and accepting of a mother's body. I tried to suck in
my belly anyway.

I also decided to drink a glass of wine at my earliest convenience.

DREAM PARK

Tristan had been bugging me for the better part of two weeks to take him to Dream Park. The name brings about visions of a loftier, finer place than it actually is. Some swings, a couple of play structures, and a bench where I could sit were the notable features; it was a typical park, barely a kid's dream, much less a mother's.

I didn't want to go. I was resistant every time he mentioned going, as I knew I would be expected to run around and play whatever random game my boys thought up. It would probably require me to climb around on the wooden castle that contained numerous short doorways just begging me to bang my head on while I pretended to have fun with my kids. I had been tired lately—overworked and overcommitted—mostly by choice, of course, but that didn't make me less weary. I had put my son's request off no fewer than four times already.

Today he asked, yet again. I believe it was my guilt from repeated rejections that put me over the top. "Mom, you promised you would today," he pleaded, batting his long eyelashes at me, revealing those pale, piercing blue eyes. And I had promised. What was I thinking? Curses. Tristan, at age six, never forgot something if it was what he wanted. I resigned myself to fulfill my promise, as it would make them happy. I would keep my promise in the strictest sense of the word only. Secretly, I was glad I did not promise myself or anyone else that *I* would be required to have fun. We would go. I would sit. They were in charge of their own fun. And, they would have to stop asking me to take them to the park. I could check one more thing off my to-do list.

"Fine," I sighed. "We can go."

They cheered, "Yeah!" fists pumping up in the air. My youngest son, Kaedyn, just over two years of age, not totally sure about what was going on, cheered along based only on the enthusiasm of his brothers. Snacks and water packed; sunscreen applied. My boys climbed into the car, smiling, chatting about our upcoming adventure. I found their enthusiasm entertaining, but not contagious. I was already thinking about the baths that would be necessary when we got home. It made me more tired just thinking about it.

The drive to the park was a short one. No sooner had I stopped than Tristan bolted from the car and onto the ramp of the wooden pirate ship. "Arrgh, me mateys, I will make you walk the plank!" he attempted to close one eye and failed, resulting in a squished face where both eyes were mostly closed. He pumped his fist in an uppercut, slightly losing his balance, but catching himself from falling at the last second. I hadn't thought to worry about injuries. Perhaps I should have. I sighed again, unfastening the last of the seatbelts to free the other two impatiently waiting, still tethered to the car. "Come on, Mom! This is going to be awesome!" Tristan yelled, running toward the wooden castle.

It's going to be something, I thought, already looking for the bench.

The younger two were off. Kaedyn lay on his belly atop a swing, lifted his legs, and swung gently into the air. Laughter followed. Quentin, the middle child at four years old, ran after his older brother, arms pumping at his side, little legs moving as quickly as his body would allow. "Wait for me, Tristan!"

"Come on, Mom!" Tristan yelled, already climbing the ladder to the castle. "This is awesome!"

I held back, trailing Kaedyn, who had gotten distracted by a dandelion. They ran across the ramp between the two towers of the castle, slid down the slide, and climbed back up. "Mom, wook at me!" Quentin yelled. His arms flailed above the opening to the tube slide, only to disappear, and then appear again, still waving as he made it to the bottom, giggling.

I smiled half-heartedly. "Looks like fun, Buddy," I said, as I checked the time on my phone. We had been at the park for three whole minutes. It seemed much longer than that.

As I put the phone back in my pocket, I looked around for my toddler, who had made his way over to the pirate ship. There were multiple opportunities for him to fall off, so I quickly followed.

Tristan and Quentin noticed the two of us heading toward the ship and came running. "We can be pirates, Mom!" Tristan suggested. "You will walk the plank," he demanded. "Arrrrgggghhhh!" already claiming the captain role as his own.

"Yeah, walk da plank, Mom," Quentin mimicked, pointing at

me, a stern look on his face, which was quickly replaced with a smile. "I wuv you, Mom." He ran off following his big brother.

I smiled. As I continued to head toward the ship, I wondered how long I could feign death if I walked the plank.

Once we had all arrived and boarded the ship, I followed Kaedyn, who seemed determined to fall off every ledge available. His brothers wandered around, steering the ship and pretending to put up sails as they had seen Uncle Tony do on his sailboat. Just as I was beginning to think they had forgotten about my plank walking, I heard Tristan exclaim with authority and seriousness, "It is time to walk the plank, Mom."

"What if I don't want to walk the plank?" I questioned, "What if I have to follow Kaedyn, so he doesn't get hurt?"

"Mom, I will watch him," he patiently explained, "and you will walk the plank."

"I don't know, Buddy," I hesitated. "I'm not sure about your plan."

He paused, the wheels in his head turning, "Well, then you will go to jail," he finally decided. He took my arm, and we left the ship heading back over to the castle. I almost made a comment about the ship being in water, and we were walking, the logic of our pretend situation seeming to elude him, but I thought better of it. I turned to check on Kaedyn, but the other two boys followed, excited at the prospect of seeing what Tristan had in mind. I was kind of curious, too, so I played along.

I was being put in jail. Actually, I was kind of looking forward to it, as I assumed, incorrectly, that I would be left alone. I climbed the ladder to the castle fully ready to serve my sentence. The only entrance to the room deemed "jail," though, was a three-foot-diameter tube about twelve feet long. "Really?" I muttered, as my jailer stood beside me pointing the way.

"This way," Tristan demanded gruffly, pointing down the tube. The severity of his voice in no way matched the expression on his face, as his smile widened and his eyes gleamed. A joyful giggle escaped his mouth, hopeful of the power in his finger. Despite my best efforts, I smiled back and, surprising both of us, submitted to his request.

I ducked my head, turned around, and slid through the black tube on my back, as even crawling on my hands and knees seemed not to be an option. I no sooner got into my jail, complete with bars on the windows so playing children couldn't fall out, when all three boys came following behind in quick succession. All four of us were now in an enclosed space much smaller than any room in our house, a big closet, perhaps. They all looked at me, smiling, anticipating a fun game in "jail." I smiled, and sighed, as I realized that this was indeed the worst version of jail I could imagine this afternoon. The older two sat along the wall, both touching my sides, and the youngest settled into my lap. While solitary confinement is considered a severe form of punishment, I was finding this sentence equally awful. Confinement in the form of personal space invasion—I worried about death by suffocation.

"What are we going to do in jail, Mom?" Quentin asked, snuggling in closer.

Tristan attempted to join his younger brother in my lap. "Yeah, what now, Mom?"

Kaedyn turned in my lap, elbowing his big brother in the side, and held my face in his hands, "Mom?" He also questioned our next event.

"I think..." I paused for effect. They leaned in, which I mistakenly believed was physically impossible, to hear the plan. "I'm going to tickle you all!" I screamed, as my fingers wiggled, finding sides, armpits, and knees. They moved away, screaming, laughing, and clamoring through the tunnel. I followed slowly, as army crawling seemed the fastest way I could get out of jail, giving them all a head start. Tristan escaped down the slide, and Quentin climbed down the ladder. The two-year-old waited patiently for me to let him down, as he was not brave enough to slide without me ready to catch him at the bottom.

Once on the ground, I chased, tickled, and chased some more. Once loose from my grasp, they would run, taunting, daring me to catch them. I did. Wrestling each to the ground, enough tickles to go around. Their giggles loud, their faces joyful—sweat beading on their little faces, light reflected, full of life. I found myself smiling despite my best efforts to resist. They all ran into the pirate ship to hide. I pretended I had no idea where they went.

After a short pause, I followed and chased, screams erupting as their hiding place was discovered. I, too, giggled and yelled, sweat beading on my face, smiling.

I had been suckered into playing. I finally admitted defeat and decided to play. It's what they wanted, and I came to make them happy. Why was I resisting making them happy? Why was I resisting *being* happy?

We took a break from our game of chase. Kaedyn found a bug

to inspect. The older two raced to the fence. I headed toward the swing set.

And so I found myself on the swing, wind blowing through my hair, legs in front of me pointing toward a beautiful blue sky dotted with white, cloudy puffs. I smiled. I breathed deep and pumped my legs higher, pulling back with my arms on the sticky chain. I exhaled, and with it, the stress bunched in my shoulders loosened a bit. With each swing, I felt higher, more playful. With every swing I became more liberated from my grumpy. I even felt less tired than when we had arrived. What had been my reason for not wanting to bring my kids to the park? The reason, whatever it was, now seemed foolish, misguided, and insignificant.

I learned I needed to get over my to-do list (containing many, many things less important than my children). My children knew how to laugh, play, and just be. They knew, better than I did, exactly what I needed. I needed to act like a pirate. I needed to climb into a space just a bit too small. I needed to chase and wrestle. I needed to swing and feel the wind in my hair. I needed to just be.

I checked my phone, surprised at how much time had passed since the last time I looked. I picked up Kaedyn, who was now playing with a pile of dirt, and headed toward the car. I buckled him in.

"Tristan and Quentin, it's time to go!" I yelled.

"Neverrrr!" Tristan yelled from his hiding spot in the tire pile, just his little arm could be seen pumping up into the air.

"Neverrrr!" an echo from his younger brother, whose matching fist, also, appeared in the air. They both giggled. I smiled.

"Neverrr is the next time we'll come to the park if you don't get over here right now," was my response. I smiled at my own wit as I heard Tristan sigh like his mother from within the tires. They came running.

Little did they know I was planning a return to Dream Park. I was going to use my kids as an excuse to play again soon.

POPCORN

The scent of hot oil filled the kitchen as kernels rattled in the pan. At our house, popcorn wasn't just a snack—it was a way of life. We ate it when we were hungry, when we were full, and when there was nothing else to do. It was more than food—it was comfort, routine, and home.

We were serious popcorn consumers growing up. It was a great snack—a whole grain, cheap, easy to make, and delicious. Mom made one dinner. If you didn't like it, you just had to deal with it. A couple of my brothers were picky, so on nights when it seemed they didn't eat much, we would have popcorn for a snack in part to fill unsatisfied bellies. It was also a typical Saturday evening treat to be had after taking showers, putting on pajamas, and while enjoying *The Muppet Show*. On Sundays, sometimes Mom would make us a big bowl of popcorn with the air popper at the beginning of an unstructured afternoon, deemed the remaining meal of the day, and then we were left to fend for ourselves if we wanted something else.

Popcorn was such a staple at our house that it was one of only two things my dad knew how to make in the kitchen. I loved watching him get out the big kettle, pour in some oil, and know just when to stir it, the smell of hot oil filling the kitchen. Dad would shake the pot, and we would wait, anticipation building. The first sounds of individual popping led quickly to the sound of a rapid-fire cacophony against the kettle's lid, the familiar sound surrounding the unfamiliar sight of Dad by the stove. Such was his lack of cooking prowess, I would marvel at how he could shake the pan and pour out only the popped kernels and leave in the unpopped ones to keep cooking. He would then put a touch of salt on the popcorn between pours. Before too long, the big family bowl was filled and small containers were doled out to each of us, to be refilled over and over as necessary throughout the evening. However, Dad got to hang onto the big bowl, King of the Popcorn.

Popcorn was such a staple in our house that even in our family pictures, it sometimes made an appearance. One of my favorites captures a rare moment—my dad, seemingly dethroned. It is remarkable for several reasons. There's the obvious difference in size. We are sitting next to each other, elbows touching, on the couch. I'm two years old, and Dad is thirty-four. For some reason, though, I'm holding onto the big bowl of popcorn, a light orange, large plastic tub of perhaps three gallons. It's a serious bowl meant to raise the dough of multiple loaves of bread, or to bring in many quarts of fresh green beans from the garden, or the day's requirement of a noteworthy volume of popcorn for this family of three. Dad, on the other hand, is holding onto my popcorn serving size at the time, a mini bread loaf pan with perhaps a volume of one cup. He's holding it with only two fingers and a thumb, as his hands are too large for more than that.

The juxtaposition of the little kid holding the big bowl while the big man holds the little bowl would be a cute picture by itself. I, however, am hanging onto the bowl, which takes up my entire lap and a bit more, with one chubby hand while the other is shoving a fistful of popcorn into my mouth, joy in my blue eyes, blonde wispy hair askew, obviously enjoying my popcorn snack to its true potential. Dad, however, is much more serious, seeming to have put just one kernel into his mouth—the size of his bowl dictating that he must savor every piece. His piercing blue eyes and still-dark brown hair seem not terribly amused at the turn of events, as popcorn is his favorite snack as well.

Not to be outdone by the focus of the picture is the explosion of patterns, placing the picture firmly in history. Dad is wearing a red and white plaid shirt, likely ending his day after spending most of it working on the family farm. We are sitting on a couch from the 1970s, a classic brown and orange leaf pattern, with a fake velvet texture you can just about see, and I can still feel. Finally, competing with the rest of them, is the gold and white vintage floral-patterned wallpaper in the background, its fanciness matching nothing else in the room. It's one of my favorite pictures of Dad and me. That picture reminds me not just of how much we loved popcorn, but how it was one of the few things that could flip the usual order of things in our house, even if just for a moment.

Popcorn was such a voluminous snack at home that when I had popcorn at someone else's house for the first time, I expected the same warm, endless supply. I was in for a surprise. We were getting popcorn to eat for our movie. I was spending the night at my friend's house, which would have been enough excitement for my fourth-grade self, but now we were going to have popcorn for a snack. *Microwave* popcorn. An unheard-of treat at our house, as it would take entirely too many bags to satisfy us all at the expected rate of consumption we knew and loved. My friend only had one brother, though, so my impression was that microwave popcorn was a regular occurrence at her house.

My excitement was short-lived, however, when her mom came in with just one bag of popcorn. One bag of popcorn. *Three* bowls. She divided the popcorn among them and gave one to each of us. My tiny bowl seemed more like a popcorn appetizer. I hoped she was going to make more, as the amount of popcorn normally eaten for snacks at my house was dramatically different than the amount doled out for me here. My fears were realized when she said, "Have fun, girls," and walked out, leaving us alone for the rest of the evening.

I hesitated before eating my first piece, savoring its buttery taste. Its fake butter flavor melted in my mouth and left grease on my hands. I had another. Amazing. One more piece of heaven gone quickly. All too soon, though, my bowl was empty. I was still hungry. Unsatisfied. A popcorn snack was something very different at someone else's house. Delicious in its own right, but like the well-plated, tiny appetizer at a fancy restaurant, I was left wanting for the main course, which never came.

Popcorn continues to be a staple in our house—made for movies, Sundays when I don't want to cook, and after meals that are only tolerated. When my boys have friends over, popcorn has become the typical snack provided, as a table full of teenage boys needs something to eat that is cheap, easy, and delicious to match the welcome regularity of their visits. I routinely use our current popcorn-making method, a Kettle Crazy turnstile popper, which requires less precision on my part in comparison to the kettle Dad used in my childhood. Based on my observations, it seems their households may not consume the volume of popcorn that was commonplace in my house of origin. However, I love the sound of laughter as they play their games, eating a popcorn snack, on the dining room table. Maybe not every house treats popcorn as a full-fledged meal. But in sharing it with my boys and their friends, I hope I'm passing down more than just a snack. I hope I'm giving them a little taste of home.

BREAKFAST STORY

At breakfast after church, we had been chatting about the most recent funeral. Stan had been an older gentleman with a large family, the father of a friend of my mother's. Dad noted that he had been known to frequent funerals, so there were many people there to return the favor. Stan was also known for being a frequent attendee at funeral lunches, so they had to set up extra tables in the Activity Center for those attending in remembrance of Stan. As the last of the scrambled eggs were getting picked out of the pan, the discussion eventually changed to a story shared at the funeral home earlier that week.

Stan had been diagnosed with liver and lung cancer six months earlier. At age eighty-seven, he had decided it was too late in life to treat it. "Live well for a little time instead of poorly for a long time" was the route he had decided to take. Stan wanted to be able to live long enough to take care of his business and say his good-byes, but not so long that he would become a burden to his family.

Dad settled in and relayed the story, "At Christmas time, everyone in the family made the trip home. The atmosphere was both joyous and bittersweet, as all knew Stan would not be with them the following Christmas. The house was full of food and family, story-telling and socializing. The grandkids played loudly, and everyone caught up on the highlights of the year. Those he loved most sur-rounded Stan.

"As the afternoon wore on, Stan excused himself to go take a nap. His daughter, your mother's friend, began scolding him. 'Dad, everyone came here to be with you. Don't you want to spend as much time with us as you can?'

"He turned slowly, eyes glistening with tears, 'I just need a min-ute,' and he shuffled off to his room. His children and their spouses grew quiet, and your mother's friend stood slightly embarrassed and emotional, as it was evident to all that Stan was fully aware of just how little time he had left. They had all made it a point to come home to celebrate together one last time. Death had been tapping Stan on the shoulder for the two months since his diagnosis, howev-er. He, too, was celebrating one last time—but was fully aware it was only *he* who would be gone from future gatherings. The moment was bittersweet."

My father finished the story. My infant son grabbed my hair, which made me yelp and him giggle. My older two boys were wres-tling loudly in the living room. As my mother started to stack the breakfast dishes, Dad grew uncharacteristically quiet. He glanced over his shoulder at my boys, and as he turned, I could see his eyes glance into the future. Death. It was a reminder at the most recent funeral, more real to him at age sixty-seven than it was a few years ago. I thought I saw a tear glistening in his eyes as the story hit home. I smiled. For both of us, the moment was bittersweet.

FOLDING CLOTHES

"All of my grey T-shirts are folded backward," I complained. "How will I know which one I'm grabbing?"

"But are they folded?" he commented. "I completed the task," his eyes daring me to fire him from the mundane job I had asked him to do. "Your way isn't the only way to do it, you know."

Taunting me in their sameness, the eight grey T-shirts on the week's laundry pile sat on the floor. One looking just like the other.

I needed to stop buying grey T-shirts.

I was so tired.

We had hit a tipping point. I was again attempting to do more things than I had the time or energy to do. Somewhere between baby number two and three, I had lost control. The laundry was winning. It was everywhere—piles of laundry near the washer and dryer, in the living room, piled on my dresser, and a load yet to be washed—all taunting me. A load of infant clothes always seemed normal-sized going into the washer but came out containing just shy of ten million items. Onesie after onesie, I folded and folded, yet the basket never emptied. And the socks—adorable, infuriating little socks—somehow wormed their way into every other piece of clothing. I'd spend thirty minutes folding, only to feel further behind, as if I were drowning in 50/50 cotton.

We needed to wash clothes, though, as the Midwest could be particularly brutal three seasons out of the year if we chose to stop wearing them. Frequently, though, I found myself sorting through the basket in the morning to find my track practice clothes or a change of clothes for one of the boys, which just resulted in unveiled frustration, clothes chaos, and frequent swearing. I needed help. I needed Jay to notice my suffering. But my loud sighs, aggressively dropped baskets, and general irritation while folding had gone completely ignored.

Finally, tired of my subtleties going unnoticed, I asked him, "Do you think you could help me fold clothes?" I pointed at the baskets surrounding me. "Like on a regular basis. Not just right now. Though I also mean right now. I can't keep up. So many little clothes." I pointed to one of the full baskets of evidence before me. "I'm dying, which sounds dramatic, but it's true." I yawned, happy my body felt compelled to verify my argument.

"Death. Hmmm. That does sound kinda dramatic. I can probably help if it'll help you avoid death. I mean, who would nurse the baby?"

I rolled my eyes and threw a clean sweatshirt at him. "Yes. We need to keep the baby fed." I pushed one of the baskets his way. "The question begs to be asked, however, if the father is currently critical to the operation of the house? The scale is definitely leaning toward

'No,' so you'd better make yourself useful."

He smirked and grabbed a shirt. We folded in relative silence for a while. The children watched a show while the baskets emptied slowly.

As a coach, I had acquired a larger than average collection of grey T-shirts, some for the school I coached for and others for the town I lived in who were sports rivals. I also had a grey one from college, where I lived in a dorm legitimately called Weed Living Center, whose saying was suggestive of drug use. When grabbing a shirt, I always looked at the front picture to make sure I was wearing the correct one in the correct location. It didn't take long before I realized Jay was folding my T-shirts wrong, picture facing in, so I didn't know which one I would be grabbing unless I unfolded it. Perhaps needing to unfold several before finding one I could take to school.

"Um, please keep folding," I started, wanting to make my primary focus known. "But could you make sure I can see the picture on my T-shirts? Especially the grey ones," I asked gently.

"For the record, you have a lot of grey T-shirts. Perhaps you could pick a different color."

"I will take it into consideration, but for now, it's what I have to wear. Could you fold them differently?"

He sighed. "And what, exactly, is the problem with how I'm folding them?"

"I can't see the picture. Will you fold them so the picture is showing? That's the right way."

He bristled. "Perhaps you should let me do it the way I want to. You want me to fold it, but you think it has to be done your way. It's laundry. There's more than one way to fold it." He turned to face me. "You can either have it done my way, or you can do it yourself." He smiled, daring me to pick, wanting me to fire him and do it all myself. All the while knowing that I was getting all kinds of twitchy at the thought of him folding all of my T-shirts front side in if I continued to need his help. Knowing him, he would now do so on purpose, just to annoy me, and to prove his point for the foreseeable future.

I was so tired.

"Fine. Do it wrong." I sighed. "I'll just refold my pile when you're done. And *for the record*, I find you irritating."

As the weeks went on, my suspicions were realized. Taunting me in their sameness, the large pile of grey T-shirts on each week's laundry pile sat on the floor. One looking just like the other. Picture folded in just to prove a point.

I needed to stop buying grey T-shirts.

Jay would listen to me sigh loudly and then watch as I picked them up, daring me with his eyes to find fault in his folding. Jay leaned back, arms crossed, watching me sigh over the pile. The smirk said it all. He was winning. Were I to complain, he would get out of folding duty permanently due to my need to be right, which is what he was hoping. If I just let the pile of grey T-shirts sit as folded and take care of them without comment, then he was winning the ongoing war.

I vowed to both keep my mouth shut and to change the infant's socks at a regularity yet to be seen. Two could play in this game.

As time went on, we deemed the boys finally big enough to sort and fold along with their dad. One would think that being the only girl in the house would mean all of the girl clothes ended up in my pile. One would be wrong.

For instance, there was the time my grey dress (I'm nothing if not consistent) ended up in Jay's pile. I could maybe see based on the feel of the cloth how they might, maybe (it's a stretch, though), think it might be a T-shirt. But not really.

"Guys, really?!" Jay held up the article of clothing in question. "It's a dress. Like not even close. I should put it on and make you look at me," he dared, as everyone got an image of Dad's XL frame in Mom's medium-sized dress.

Quentin started to giggle, changing positions for a better look, hoping he would do it.

I grabbed it away, not sure if he was kidding. "Come on, guys. Are you even trying? It's obviously a dress. I'm obviously the only girl in the house. Let's get better at folding laundry," I instructed. "If you keep being terrible at it, you'll be given more practice." I smirked, knowing that at least one of the boys, a disciple of his father, was trying to get fired from this new job he was not enjoying.

"There's a lot of grey laundry, Mom," Quentin observed.

Jay chuckled, going through the rest of his pile for errant dresses.

I pushed Jay, acknowledging his taunting. "So I've been told, Buddy," I conceded, deciding I needed to go through my pile as well,

I'm hoping to delay folding the laundry, mine or anyone else's, for as long as possible. I can refold just my own clothes, which is faster than folding all of them. There's still a best way to fold T-shirts, obviously. But I've decided having my clothes folded "good enough" is worth the time and energy saved. Jay and the boys still frequently fold my shirts incorrectly or put them in the wrong pile. I still sigh. But I also don't fold an entire family's laundry anymore, so I'm calling it a win.

ROOFING SON

It was after Sunday breakfast. Dad proposed, "What do you think about Tristan working with me this summer?"

The thought had never crossed my mind.

My firstborn seemed to be too young, but he was, at twelve, already a year older than I was when I started working. He was a shocking seven years past the ripe old age of five, my youngest brother's first experience on the roof. I felt like we'd be almost coddling him if we said no.

"I mean, I don't work quite as many hours as I used to. And I'm pickier about the jobs I take, but I could use another hand this summer and thought he might be good at it. Why don't you two talk it over and let me know?"

I looked at Jay, eyebrow raised, questioning. He, too, had spent two summers working with Dad in college. We both had first-hand knowledge of the kinds of things Tristan would be doing. This was both a good and a bad thing. We had both done some jobs with questionable safety precautions. "Is this OSHA approved?" was a periodic question my brothers and I asked before completing a task where we wondered at the safety measures of Dad's plan. While there weren't many injuries during Dad's roofing career, it seems there were several stories to be told where things worked out in the end, but you weren't quite sure it was going to work out that way in the middle of the tale. Dad was over seventy now, though, and his jobs had shrunk as his age increased, less steep, less risky.

While his proposal caused me pause initially, Jay and I had also both learned many useful skills, which had helped us complete and save money with several DIY projects at our house. Those paled in comparison, though, to the life lessons we each developed through our work with Dad and his various crews. There was a growing part of me that didn't want to rob Tristan of the opportunity to learn those lessons, on the roof and in other places, which only Dad could impart in his unique way.

"Hey, Tristan, come in here for a minute," Jay called.

He came jogging out of the living room. "Yeah?"

"What would you think about working with Papa a bit this summer?"

Tristan was a bit surprised by the offer and paused.

"I'd pay you," Dad offered, making sure he knew the most important detail.

As the dollar signs danced in his pale blue eyes, the same color as his Papa's, a smile broke out on Tristan's face. "Yeah! I could do that.

❄   ❄   ❄

On his first day of work, Tristan and I pulled into Mom and Dad's driveway at 7:12 to make sure he was on time for a 7:15 departure. I had loaned him some lunch money, at no interest (though I made him listen to me explain what that meant), to be paid back on his first payday. Jay had let him know about ordering lunch, asking questions, and working hard the night before. Jay had also told him about some of Dad's lingo, informing him that a "diddly knife" was actually a utility knife. I had made him put on sunscreen before we left and warned him about drinking enough water. I was being a cautious-hovering-overbearing mother, and I knew it, but I couldn't stop myself.

Tristan, listening, nodded and tried, only sometimes successfully, not to roll his eyes.

I stopped the car at the house. Tristan opened the door. "Have fun. Work hard. Be a good listener," I called as final instructions as Tristan got out.

"Yeah, I will," he barely paused.

"I love you," I tried to get in before the car door shut.

"Love you, too." I caught his mumble as the door shut, and he started down the hill toward the barn. My boy-man sauntered down the hill, every bit the almost teenager he was. As I watched him walk to the truck, the inward curve of his shoulder and slight tilt of his head hinted at his nervousness.

Dad was loading the truck. Steve, his current employee, grabbed his cooler. Tristan stood by the truck, unsure what to do, leaning on the sideboard. His focus changed, and I could tell Dad was giving him a task. He went into the barn and then loaded a box of screws.

They all piled in. The truck started.

Dad backed up. I found myself getting out my phone. *Who am I?! When did you become this kind of mom? This is so ridiculous!* I said to myself.

I got ready to take a picture.

They drove by me slowly. Dad driving, Tristan in the middle—where he would inevitably learn how to drive a stick shift—and Steve by the window. I knew I was witnessing a rite of passage.

The roofer's daughter now had a roofing son.

Life Lessons from the Peaks and Valleys

And so it is, as my father undoubtedly intended, in attending funeral after funeral and being reminded of death on a regular basis throughout my childhood, that I learned how to truly live. It is this gift from my father, given to him by his family, for which I am the most thankful. It is beginning with the end in mind, as every good teacher knows, that I try to approach life. As a result of my many conversations with my father on the subject, I have pondered the rather morbid thought of being diagnosed with an illness or injury that would cut my life short and have come to the conclusion, at least for now, that there aren't very many changes I would make. My marginally clean house would get dirtier, and we'd hire someone to clean it. I'd travel to the current homes of my brothers, with a bit more urgency to visit the people I love. My boys and I would take a few more day trips. I would make more time to go on dates with my husband and not worry, to his delight, about the size of the bill at the end of the night.

Many things would stay the same, however. I would continue to stop whatever I'm doing and have a dance party in the kitchen with my boys when the mood strikes us. I would continue to kiss my husband every morning and night and never leave his side without saying "I love you" and meaning it. We would share our "best" of the day, along with our "prayers and thankfuls", before going to bed at night, along with hugs and snuggles. I would cook meals and make my boys eat their vegetables, at least some of them, before they could have dessert. I would go to church with my family and eat breakfast with my parents every Sunday to talk about the past week and discover important life lessons in our discussions. Perhaps I would even continue to work in my middle school classroom as long as possible, as I love my kids and the people I work with. Sitting at home and dwelling on an illness, stuck with my fears and my insecurities, seems neither positive for me nor for those around me. I would make the most of the time I had with my family at the end of the day, as I always do.

Some day my funeral will happen, even as I try to avoid it. Perhaps things will be very much the same as they usually are in my family. Perhaps my children will have their own idea of what a funeral should be like. I do know that I don't have much control over what happens. I will be dead, so I will no longer have control issues, which actually makes me smile. It is my hope, however, that when I am surrounded by flowers and pictures of my life, including my *horrible* middle school pictures with my expertly-teased hair-do, that many people walk through the doors with a story in their heart, a tear in their eye, and a smile on their face at a life well lived. Regardless of the details of the day itself, I hope that my children, family, and friends will find me to have been a loving, faith-filled woman. They will tell stories. They will laugh. They will cry. They will know how much I love them. They will celebrate my life—one of a mother, a wife, and a roofer's daughter.

Book Club Exercises for Each Section

1. CHILDHOOD AND FAMILY PROJECTS

Exercise: Reflect on Your Family's Legacy

- Think of a significant project or tradition in your family. It could be something tangible, like building a structure or cooking together, or intangible, like storytelling or a shared holiday tradition.

- Write a short paragraph describing this project or tradition. Consider these questions:

  - Who participated in it, and what roles did they play?

  - What values or lessons did it teach you?

  - How does this tradition or project represent your family's identity?

- If possible, take a photo, sketch, or create a keepsake that represents this memory to preserve it for future generations.

2. ADULTHOOD AND LIFE LESSONS

EXERCISE: BALANCING RESPONSIBILITIES

- Create a "Life Balance Chart." Divide a piece of paper into four quadrants labeled: *Work*, *Relationships*, *Personal Growth*, and *Fun/Leisure*.

- Reflect on how you currently allocate time to each area in a typical week. Mark approximate hours or activities in each quadrant.

- Now ask yourself:

  - Which quadrant feels neglected, and why?

  - What's one small change you could make this week to create more balance?

- Implement your change and journal about how it affects your week.

3. MOTHERHOOD AND PERSPECTIVE

EXERCISE: TEACH A LIFE LESSON

- Think about a skill, lesson, or value you want to pass on to your children (or someone younger in your life).

- Write down a step-by-step guide for teaching this lesson. It could be practical, like cooking a family recipe, or emotional, like practicing gratitude.

- Next, reflect:
  - How did you learn this skill or value yourself? Who taught it to you?
  - What do you hope the person you teach will take away from this experience?
- Plan a time to teach it and write a few sentences afterward about how it went.

4. GENERAL BONUS EXERCISE

THE ROOFTOP REFLECTION

- Imagine yourself standing on a symbolic "rooftop" where you can see the big picture of your life.
- Answer these questions:
  - What are you most proud of when looking back on your "foundation" (childhood)?
  - What unfinished "projects" or goals still await completion?
  - How will you ensure the structure of your life remains strong for years to come?
- Write a short reflection or sketch your vision of this rooftop view.